Improving your Human–Computer Interface

4301 THIRD STREET
TILLAMOOK, OREGON 97141
PH 503.842.8222

BCS Practitioner Series

Series Editor: Ray Welland

Improving your Human—Computer Interface

A practical technique

Andrew Monk, Peter Wright, Jeanne Haber
and Lora Davenport

Prentice Hall

New York   London   Toronto   Sydney   Tokyo   Singapore

First published 1993 by
Prentice Hall International (UK) Ltd
Campus 400, Maylands Avenue
Hemel Hempstead
Hertfordshire, HP2 7EZ
A division of
Simon & Schuster International Group

Typeset in 10½/12 pt Times Roman
by MHL Typesetting Ltd, Coventry

Printed and bound in Great Britain by
Dotesios Limited, Trowbridge, Wiltshire

Library of Congress Cataloging-in-Publication Data

Improving your human—computer interface: a practical technique /
   Andrew Monk ... [et al.].
     p. cm. — (BCS practitioner series)
   Includes bibliographical references and index.
   ISBN 0-13-010034-X (pbk)
   1. Human—computer interaction.   2. User interfaces (Computer
systems)   I. Monk, Andrew.   II. Series.
QA76.9.H85I57   1993
005.1'2—dc20   92-38730
                                                              CIP

British Library Cataloguing in Publication Data

A catalogue record for this book is available from
the British Library

ISBN 13-010034-X (pbk)

1 2 3 4 5   97 96 95 94 93

Contents

Editorial preface

The aim of the BCS Practitioner Series is to produce books which are relevant for practising computer professionals across the whole spectrum of Information Technology activities. We want to encourage practitioners to share their practical experience of methods and applications with fellow professionals. We also seek to disseminate information in a form which is suitable for the practitioner who often has only limited time to read widely within new subject areas or to assimilate research findings.

The role of the BCS is to provide advice on the suitability of books for the Series, via the Editorial Panel, and to provide a pool of potential authors upon which we can draw. Our objective is that this Series will reinforce the drive within the BCS to increase professional standards in IT. The other partner in this venture, Prentice Hall, provides the publishing expertise and international marketing capabilities of a leading publisher in the computing field.

The response when we set up the Series was extremely encouraging. However, the success of the Series depends on there being practitioners who want to learn, as well as those who feel they have something to offer! The Series is under continual development and we are always looking for ideas for new topics and feedback on how further to improve the usefulness of the Series. If you are interested in writing for the Series then please contact us.

Costly changes can be avoided if usability problems can be detected early in the design of a human—computer interface. This book offers practical advice on how to do this using Cooperative Evaluation. The authors have drawn heavily on their experience of teaching the technique to designers without human factors training and its use at Information Dimensions Inc., Ohio. It includes a step-by-step guide to its use with checklists designed to be photocopied and used to run evaluation sessions.

Ray Welland
Computing Science Department, University of Glasgow

Editorial Panel Members
Frank Bott (UCW, Aberystwyth), Dermot Browne (KPMG Management Consulting), Nic Holt (ICL), Trevor King (Praxis Systems Plc), Tom Lake (GLOSSA), Kathy Spurr (Analysis and Design Consultants), Mario Wolczko (University of Manchester)

Preface

This book describes how to use Cooperative Evaluation. Cooperative Evaluation is a technique to improve a user interface specification by detecting possible usability problems in an early prototype or partial simulation. It sets down procedures by which a designer can work with the sort of people who will ultimately use the software in their daily work, so that together they can identify potential problems and their solutions.

The last few years have seen the facilities available to the designer of user interface software increase beyond recognition. New graphical display technologies, input devices and the software libraries and tool kits to use them have increased the possibilities open to the designer manyfold. This new freedom is not all good news. It increases the possibilities for innovative new solutions to old problems but at the same time introduces new problems of complexity. Having more freedom means more opportunity to make the wrong decision. There is a need for techniques to test and improve a prototype user interface specification so that designers can have the same confidence in the user interface that they have in other aspects of the software.

The ultimate aim of research in human−computer interaction is to assist design and there have been a number of projects to translate the results of this research into methods to be used by practitioners. Unfortunately, many of these methods involve a large commitment of resources in terms of manpower and project time.

In many companies management still have to be convinced that human factors techniques are cost effective and are not willing to take the risk involved in committing the resources necessary for these 'expensive' techniques. The philosophy of this book is that there is a place for 'discount methods' requiring only limited resources. Cooperative Evaluation is just such a method. Starting with a procedure that is demonstrably effective at a very low cost, is a low risk option and so more acceptable to management.

The major costs to be minimised are:

(a) staff and training and
(b) the time and resources needed to actually carry out the procedure.

Cooperative Evaluation minimises the first cost because it can be carried out by designers with little or no knowledge of human factors after only a minimal amount of training. Using designers as evaluators also minimises the second cost as it cuts out the need for the designer to brief the evaluator and for the evaluator to report back to the designer.

Cooperative Evaluation was developed at York University, first as a research tool. As its potential as a practical evaluation technique became apparent we began 'selling' it to industry. In 1989 Lora Davenport heard a talk about it by Peter Wright at the CHI'89 conference in Texas. She and Jeanne Haber used it at Information Dimensions Inc. Since then the manual describing it has been refined and distributed to many companies and the technique presented at several international conferences. This book is the result of all that experience.

Chapter 1 gives the background to the method: why it is necessary to design user interfaces by progressive refinement; why users have to be a part of this process; and why Cooperative Evaluation takes the particular form that it does. There is also a discussion of the alternatives and the limitations of the technique.

Chapter 2 is a 'how to' manual written for designers with little or no formal background in human factors. It describes the steps to be taken to make it possible for a designer to identify problems in a putative design. This includes how to recruit users; how to select tasks for them to do; how to encourage the user to make constructive comments as they work; and how to record and interpret what ensues.

Chapter 3 describes the steps Information Dimensions Inc. went through in order to incorporate Cooperative Evaluation into the procedures used by the company; how they gained access to users; trained designers; and obtained the confidence of their management.

Chapter 4 describes the validation of the procedure in two experiments at the University of York. Experiment 1 demonstrates the effectiveness of the procedure in terms of the probability of detecting a problem. Experiment 2 demonstrates that the procedure is more effective when used by the designers of the user interface being examined than by equivalent others.

All four authors have considerable experience, both of using Cooperative Evaluation and of teaching its use to others. Perhaps the most striking thing that emerges from this experience is the surprises designers experience each time Cooperative Evaluation is used. The users are working to complete tasks set by the designer yet they say and do things quite contrary to expectation. If you are convinced that your design is perfect and you are just looking for a technique to confirm your opinion Cooperative Evaluation is not for you. If, on the other hand, you wish to change and improve your design and are willing to learn from these surprises then read on.

Acknowledgements

Cooperative Evaluation was developed while the first two authors were working on a UK Science and Engineering Research Council supported project, 'Formal specification linked with evaluation in the iterative design of interactive systems'. We would like to acknowledge the help of our colleagues on that project, Nick Hammond, Michael Harrison, Colin Runciman and Harold Thimbleby as well as all our other colleagues who have commented on the work in the departments of Psychology and Computer Science at the University of York. In particular, we should mention Tom Carey of the University of Guelph, Canada, who was spending a year at York at the time and who made a major contribution to the writing of the original York Manual. We should also thank the several classes of Computer Science students who used the manual in its various forms and whose comments allowed us to practise what we preach and improve our own product by participatory design.

The following terms are known to be trademarks:
Hypercard is a trademark of Apple Computer Inc.
Toolbook is a trademark of Asymetrics Inc.

1 An introduction to Cooperative Evaluation

1.1 Topics covered in this chapter

- How to use this book
- Why users need to be involved in design and why you need a prototype
- Forms a prototype can take
- When to involve users in design
- What is required to evaluate a prototype?
- How does Cooperative Evaluation work?
- Other techniques
- Cooperative Evaluation as participatory design

This book is about Cooperative Evaluation, a technique for getting feedback to identify points where a prototype design could be changed to make it more usable. Cooperative Evaluation involves users in design by having them complete tasks set by the designer; at the same time they are encouraged to explain what they are doing and any difficulties they have. Its distinctive features are:

- it is practical — it can be carried out by designers with very little training and without expensive facilities such as 'usability laboratories';
- it is cost effective in that it reveals important usability problems in a relatively short time;
- it is for use with early designs and prototypes that may not be complete;
- it brings together designer and user in a cooperative context; the user completes work using the prototype and is encouraged to think aloud about the problems experienced.

Chapter 2 is a self-contained 'how to' manual, written for designers, that describes the technique, how to set up an evaluation session and how to interpret the results. This first chapter provides some background. Chapter 3 is a case study of the use of Cooperative Evaluation at Information Dimensions Inc. in Ohio. Chapter 4 describes two experiments that examine the validity of the technique.

1.2   How to use this book

This is a book primarily for practitioners:

>project managers,
>software engineers,
>technical authors,
>software developers and designers.

For this reason we have kept it as brief as possible. Even so, a busy manager or designer may not have time to read it from Chapter 1 through to Chapter 4. Such readers may find it better to read Chapters 2 and 3 first. These chapters contain all the information needed to start using the technique. Appendix 1 is a run-time guide. This is an abridged version of Chapter 2 with checklists that can be used while actually running an evaluation session. One can then return to the other chapters for a deeper understanding of the technique, after having used it.

Human factors personnel who want to train designers to use Cooperative Evaluation can use Chapter 2 and Appendix 1 as basic teaching material. Chapter 2 stands on its own as a self-contained instruction manual for designers. The transcripts from a real Cooperative Evaluation session printed as Appendix 2 may also be useful in generating exercises for use in training.

University and college lecturers designing practical exercises on usability testing can similarly use Chapter 2 and Appendices 1 and 2. The other chapters and the bibliography also make the book useful as an accessible case study in a course on the theory of usability testing.

1.3   Why users need to be involved in design and why you need a prototype

Synopsis

Q. Why do we have to involve users in design?

A. There is a problem of communication.

The purpose of a user interface is to communicate with the user. However, the designer and the user have quite different backgrounds and concerns, so it is very difficult for the designer to predict what effect some design decision will have on a user's behaviour. A prototype can provide the necessary common ground. It is relatively easy to observe users working with a prototype and understand the problems they are having.

Terms such as 'prototype', 'involving users' and 'evaluation' have very negative connotations for many designers. This is because the procedures involving users or prototypes adopted in many organisations have not been constructive. In such organisations 'evaluation' means judging whether the final product is good or bad. There may be a place for this kind of evaluation as quality assurance but it is not much use to a designer. A designer needs constructive evaluation, that is, feedback about how the design can be improved.

Before going any further we will illustrate in an example how prototypes and users can be utilised constructively. This comes from a now classic paper in the human—computer interaction literature. The two authors of this paper, John Gould and Clayton Lewis, were at the time research scientists at the IBM Thomas J. Watson Research Laboratories in York Town Heights, New York. The paper is entitled 'Designing for usability: key principles and what designers think'. It includes, as a case study, a description of the work they did to develop the user interface for a voice messaging system ADS, the Audio Distribution System. This system, which has since been marketed all over the world, allows a user to compose a voice message and then send it to some other individual's message box where it waits for their attention. Its main function is similar to that of the centrally located electronic voice mail and answerphones now installed in many organisations, but in the early 1980s, when this work was done, these were not generally available. ADS is accessed through an ordinary touch-tone telephone with extra characters engraved on the buttons.

Gould and Lewis describe a number of improvements they were able to make by involving users in the design process. Their general procedure was to give a few users a task and to ask them to say and to demonstrate what they would do to complete it. For example, they might have been instructed:

> 'You have arranged to meet Frank Howard for lunch at 12.30. Use ADS to tell him you will be 30 minutes late.'

One of the problems they relate in their paper illustrates very clearly how difficult it is to predict in advance how users will behave. In all the early prototypes the sequence for creating a message was initiated by pressing the '7' key that was also engraved 'R' for 'record'. Having completed that sequence the user then pressed the '8' key and that was engraved 'T' for transmit (see Figure 1.1, Version 1). While there were no obvious problems with this arrangement, it was decided that 'R' for 'record' and 'T' for 'transmit' might be more memorable if they were replaced by the shorter and more commonly used words 'T' for 'talk' and 'S' for 'send' (see Figure 1.1, Version 2).

When users were asked to work with early versions of this system there was a persistent tendency to 'send' before 'talking'. The system was not set up like this. A message has to be created before the recipient can be specified. The result was much confusion. For some reason, this problem did not arise with Version 1. Users found it natural to 'record' before 'transmitting'. Rather than changing the basic structure of the system the designers went back to Version 1.

Figure 1.1
Two alternatives
considered when
prototyping ADS

Version 1

1	2	3
4	5	6
7 R	8 T	9
*	O	#

R = record
T = transmit

Version 2

1	2	3
4	5	6
7 S	8 T	9
*	O	#

T = talk
S = send

After the event, one can think of a variety of possible explanations for this finding, but one can see how it might not be at all easy to predict the problem in advance. This example serves to illustrate one of the reasons why users have to be involved in design, that is, because it is very difficult to predict the effect some design decision will have on their behaviour. On the other hand, it is very easy to observe a user's behaviour when working with a prototype and to understand the problems they have.

Another reason for involving users in design is that designers have a strong tendency to design for themselves. As they are very likely to have different backgrounds to the users, and a quite different understanding of the system, this can also lead to problems. This is illustrated in the second example taken from Gould and Lewis's case study. This concerned the auditory menu used both to edit a message immediately after creating it and also to annotate a message from someone else (see Figure 1.2). Auditory menus were used throughout the system. The items in the menu were spoken to the user, 'Dial 1 to . . . , dial 2 to . . . , dial 3 to . . .'. The user then presses the appropriate button on the touch-tone telephone.

The menu in Figure 1.2 allows a user to add to the beginning of a message (prepend), to add to the end of a message (append) and to delete the message altogether. These functions could be used to change a message the user has just created as well as to annotate a message from someone else before sending it back or forwarding it to someone else. The designer had a very clear understanding of these functions in terms of the primitive editing functions:

Figure 1.2
Auditory menu used
to edit and annotate
messages in ADS

'Dial 1 to add a comment at the beginning of the message' (system prepends new material)

'Dial 2 to add a comment where you stopped listening' (system appends new material)

'Dial 3 to erase message and start over' (system deletes message) prepend, append and delete. To a programmer and frequent user of computer systems, these functions are very familiar. However, the users of ADS were managers and office personnel who only use computer systems occasionally. As Gould and Lewis soon found out, these users did not have these concepts and so did not see the tasks of annotation and editing as being equivalent. The wording of items 1 and 2 of the auditory menu only make sense if you are annotating someone else's message. The word 'comment' does not make any sense in the context of editing a message one has just created oneself. Likewise, 'start over' in item 3 of the menu is only meaningful in the context of editing and makes no sense if one is annotating someone else's message. Users had great difficulty doing the tasks set them that required using this menu. It was finally decided that the only solution was to radically change the structure of the system so that editing and annotation could be distinguished and different auditory menus used in each case.

These two examples from ADS illustrate an important point about the testing of early designs with users that is central to an understanding of Cooperative Evaluation. Involving users in design does not mean having endless meetings where some abstract specification is discussed with union representatives or management. Cooperative Evaluation requires access to people typical of those who will actually use the system, not their representatives or management. The 'discussion' revolves around the use of a concrete prototype to do specified tasks, not some abstract specification.

The reason why it is necessary to involve users in design in this way comes down to a problem of communication. One can draw a useful analogy between the designer's task and that of the author of a report. This is depicted in Figure 1.3. When writing a report one is designing an artefact that will be used, that is read, when one is not present. For this reason the author has to try and envisage the reader's thought processes and anticipate any problems they might have in advance. This is very difficult to do. What can be very helpful is to prepare a draft and have someone else read it and point out where it is obscure or awkward to read. The same thing applies to the designer of a user interface to a computer system. While the concepts to be conveyed may be simpler the artefact itself is much more complex. The designer is

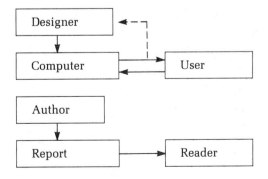

Figure 1.3
The analogy between the designer's task and that of the author of a report

communicating with the user remotely just as the author of a report is communicating remotely with the reader. However, whereas the author of a report is usually writing for people of the same background and with similar focus and motivations, the designer, on the other hand, will often have quite a different perspective of the system than the user and a much more technical background. This means that to test and improve the specification for a user interface it is necessary to observe users working with a prototype or simulation. This is equivalent to getting someone else to read a draft report, but it is much more important because of the greater potential for confusion.

In summary, users need to be involved in design because there is a problem of communication. The eventual users of a computer application are likely to have very different concerns and backgrounds to the designer. A system that is designed to make sense to the designer may not make sense to the user. Of course this difference in background also makes it difficult for the designer to talk to the user about the design. Common ground can be achieved if the specification takes the form of a prototype of some kind and the user is given some task to perform with it. By talking to the users and observing their behaviour the designer can come to understand the user's point of view and improve the specification appropriately.

1.4   Forms a prototype can take

Synopsis

Q. What is a prototype user interface?

A. A prototype is a representation of the user interface that a user can interact with, built to be changed and improved.

It might be:

    a short user guide
    a paper simulation
    a software simulation using a prototyping tool or interface generator
    an early version of the software
    the system to be replaced

Examples are given in Figure 1.4.

Cooperative Evaluation depends on the use of a prototype or simulation. This could take several forms some of which are illustrated in Figure 1.4. Several authors have suggested that the first prototyping exercise should be to prepare a brief user guide. Gould *et al.* (1987) (see Bibliography) describe how user guides were prepared for the Olympic Message System (OMS) before any code had been written. OMS is a subsequent development of ADS as a messaging system for use at the 1984 Los Angeles Olympics. The user guides were tested on appropriate user groups and rewritten to reflect the new ideas about design that arose. Interestingly, the revised guides very quickly became

Figure 1.4
Examples of forms a
prototype can take

User guides
OMS: The two user guides 'Olympic Message System User Guide'
and the 'Family and Friends User Guide' were written and tested
before coding began.

Simulations
ADS: Users pretend numeric key pad is touch-tone telephone. A
hidden operator, on telephone, observes key presses and speaks
OMS messages.

Working prototype
ADS: users work with a system though it is not complete and is
not running on the eventual target hardware/software platform.

Existing system
BASISplus: users work with some part of the system that is to
be updated.

the definitive document for specifying the user interface to OMS. That is,
they became the specification that designers referred to when they were unsure
how the user interface was supposed to work. A user guide is necessarily
user-centred and so having the user guide as a specification encourages user-
centred design. Also a brief user guide is a very accessible form of
specification. You do not need any knowledge of specialised notations or
programming languages to read it.

Another commonly used form of prototype is a simulation. Part or all of
the user interface may be simulated on paper or using some general purpose
software such as a drawing package or a hypertext authoring environment
such as HyperCard on an Apple Macintosh or Toolbook on a PC. A simulation
differs from a working prototype in that it has no real functionality. One can
still use a simulation in a technique like Cooperative Evaluation because the
tasks to be carried out by the user are specified by the designer. This makes
it possible to predict what the user is going to do and so fake the missing
functionality. An example will make this clear.

Let us say that a menu-driven enquiry system is to be tested. A subset of
the menus are written on cards as they will appear on the screen. The subset
is sufficient for the user to complete a given query, say to find the times of
flights from New York to Chicago. The first menu is put in front of the user,
who is asked to respond. If the right response is chosen that card is removed
and the next menu is provided. If the wrong response is chosen the user is
questioned about this and informed of the correct answer. In this way a
complete query can be simulated without any branching into the menu structure.
In the next iteration one might use the information gathered to provide 'screens'
additional to this linear progression. One might have cards simulating some
of the screen that might be accessed by mistake to see if the user can recognise
that the wrong choice has been made when this is done. One might also have
simulated help screens.

The first simulation where there is no branching could be achieved with a drawing package. The second would require something more complex such as hypertext authoring software. Screen builders can also be used to set up simulations quickly. Presenting the screens on a computer gives the simulation veracity. Although many designers feel that this is important, using paper is often easier and communicates to the user that the simulation really is a prototype to be changed and not some finished product the designer is seeking approval for.

Another commonly used simulation technique has come to be known as the 'Wizard-of-Oz' technique because it depends on a hidden operator. Gould and Lewis used this in their initial tests of the ADS interface. At this stage there was no software available to produce the speech messages. To get around this they used a hidden operator. The user and the designer/evaluator were in one room. Unknown to the user, there was another designer in a nearby room. When the user pressed a key the corresponding character was displayed on a screen in front of the hidden operator who had a table specifying what the system response should be. He then spoke that response in his telephone hand set and it was heard by the user. No expensive equipment was required. The keys were mocked up by masking off all but the numeric keypad on a standard keyboard and then relabelling the keys. Voice communication was achieved simply by connecting two telephone extensions. With a little ingenuity much of the functionality of many systems can be simulated by linking two microcomputers so that a hidden operator can view the user's actions and control the user's display.

The last two prototypes described in Figure 1.4 are working systems. They are classed as prototypes rather than implementations because they are there to be changed. For example, the first working prototype may be built using general purpose software and a more powerful system than the final implementation will run on. This will make it relatively easy to change. Chapter 3 describes how Cooperative Evaluation has been used at Information Dimensions Inc. (Ohio). Here the 'prototype' is the existing system. Information Dimensions Inc. are responsible for BASISplus, a text information management system. When they are about to redesign some part of this system they get users to work on tasks that involve using those functions. By observing the problems users have they are able to get ideas about what should be changed and how. In this way the current implementation is used as a prototype to be tested and improved.

1.5   When to involve users in design

Synopsis

Q. *When* in the design process can users provide useful information?

A. From start to finish.

One can distinguish three products of the design process: the requirements (what it should achieve), the specification (easily changed blueprint for testing) and the implementation (final product).

Observing users doing real work or 'representative' tasks can inform the requirements, the specification and the relationship between them.

Cooperative Evaluation is primarily to refine the specification so that it meets the requirements for usability.

This section discusses the place of Cooperation Evaluation in the design process. There are many models of system development. Many use the same terms in slightly different ways. There is also much controversy about how design should proceed. However, there is some general agreement that there are three deliverables that have to be created in this process. These are depicted in Figure 1.5. They are a requirements document, a specification and the implementation.

The requirements document defines what the system is to achieve. For example, it should have specific functions, it should run on a particular kind of personal computer, it should respond to certain queries within two seconds and it should cost such and such. One should also define user requirements in such a document. Who will use the system, what other systems have they experience of, how long should it take them to learn to use it, how fast should they be able to specify certain transactions? To do this one needs a good understanding of the tasks the user is doing, both with and without the system; thus one can think of the design of the user's job as also being part of the requirements.

The implementation is the working software that goes out the door. An implementation is very difficult to change and so, as in other engineering disciplines, implementation is preceded by the construction of a specification or blueprint. This describes what the implementation will look like and how

Requirements (what is it to achieve)
System concerns: System functionality, hardware and software platform, cost, performance
User concerns: Type of user, job design, learning time, performance

Specification (a blue print, easy to change)
System concerns: Architecture, details of functionality
User concerns: Dialogue design, details of user interface and documentation

Implementation (the working system, very difficult to change)
System concerns: Working software that follows the specification
User concerns: A new way of working

Figure 1.5
Deliverables in system development

it will work in some detail, but is much more easy to change than the implementation itself.

In this book, we are concerned with the creation of the first two deliverables, the requirements and the specification. We view prototypes and simulations as part of the specification because they are built for testing and are easy to change. A user interface is specified in terms of displays and commands and the way these combine to form a dialogue between user and computer. Because a prototype can exhibit *behaviour* it is an ideal way of doing this.

Having defined our terms we can now return to the question of when users should be involved in the design process. The answer is from start to finish. The requirements described above can only be obtained by working closely with users from the very start of the project. Initially this involves observing users in the work place in order to get an understanding of the tasks the system is to support (see the last section of this chapter for a discussion of the methods for doing this).

Cooperative Evaluation is for use later in the design process when there is an initial prototype to test. Having users work with prototypes can lead to changes to improve these initial requirements. Two examples will make this clear. ADS was initially designed as an enhanced dictation system and only secondarily as a messaging system. After all, who would want to leave someone a message when nine times out of ten one could pick up the telephone and talk directly? When the first working prototype was put into the work place it was found that these priorities were quite the wrong way round. Users of electronic mail will know that there are many occasions when it is preferable to leave a message even when you know the recipient is in the office next to you. Also for various, mainly organisational, reasons dictation over the telephone was not seen as a desirable innovation. IBM were willing to learn from this experience and the user interface was completely redesigned to reflect the change in priorities.

The problem identified here can be thought of as one of supporting the wrong task. As such it is a problem with the requirements. The requirements were modified to reflect the new priorities and the specification changed to support these new requirements.

The second example of how observing users working with a prototype can result in changes to the requirements comes from the development of OMS. This is described in a paper by Gould *et al.* (1987). The Olympic Message System (OMS) was a voice mail system to allow family and friends to send messages to Olympians and Olympians to send messages to each other. The system was accessed through booths around the Olympic Village and, for the family and friends, by telephone. The initial design, built on the functionality of ADS, included the possibility of reviewing and modifying a message before it was sent. Initial testing with family and friends indicated that this functionality was unnecessarily time-consuming. Testing the user interface with users revealed that there was a missing requirement. This was that interaction with the system over the telephone should be straightforward and brief. International calls are expensive, callers cannot afford the luxury of playing back their message. Even the time spent listening to an auditory menu and specifying that they did not want to play back the message was considered unnecessary. As a result of this early testing with potential users the design of OMS was modified to remove functions for playing back and editing a message before sending it.

This is again a problem with the requirements. There was a missing requirement, 'keep the dialogue brief'. Adding it forced changes in the specification. Cooperative Evaluation can identify problems with the requirements, as in these two examples. Its primary function, however, is to identify problems in the specification. The two earlier examples from Gould and Lewis's (1985) paper on the development of ADS illustrate the kind of changes we have in mind. In the first the specification, in the form of a simulation, was tested and found to induce the wrong behaviour in the user. Using 'T' and 'S' resulted in users trying to 'send' before they 'talked'. 'R' and 'T' generally induced the right behaviour. This change to the specification is a small detail. Though small it may have a large impact on the overall usability of this part of the system. Changing from T/S to R/T might be thought of as analogous to testing the specification for a data structure and finding that one of its fields was too small.

In the second example from the development of ADS a more radical change to the specification was suggested. The structure of the human–computer dialogue was changed so that different auditory menus could be used for editing a message that the user had just created and annotating someone else's message. This can be thought of as analogous to testing the specification of an algorithm and changing it because it does not work in some conditions.

In summary, three deliverables that have to be created in the process of building a computer application were defined. They are:

(a)   a set of requirements that have to be achieved;
(b)   a specification or blueprint that can be tested and easily changed and
(c)   the implementation that is the finished working product that cannot be easily changed.

Close involvement with users is the only way to get sufficient initial requirements to produce a good user-interface specification. Subsequent testing of the user interface specification, in the form of a partial prototype or simulation, can reveal changes that need to be made in the requirements and the specification.

Techniques such as Cooperative Evaluation that involve observing users performing tasks set by the designer are most suitable for testing the specification. Though they will sometimes show up missing or inappropriate requirements (e.g. keeping international calls brief) they cannot detect a problem in the user tasks described in the requirements. The problem of false task priorities in the initial design of ADS was only detected when a prototype was built that allowed free use. Prior testing where tasks were given to the user, as in Cooperative Evaluation, could not detect this problem. This limitation of Cooperative Evaluation will be discussed further in the penultimate section of this chapter in the context of alternative techniques.

1.6   What is required?

Synopsis

Q. What is required of a technique for testing a user interface specification?

A. The requirements of such a technique are

1. It should not need a full working system, that is, it should be possible to use it with prototypes and partial simulations.

2. It should be applicable rapidly, that is:
   (a) it should be a low cost procedure;
   (b) it should be possible for the designer to carry out the technique;
   (c) it should be natural to users and designers alike and so is easy to learn to do.

3. It should provide the maximum feedback about how the design should be changed, that is, it should provide detailed qualitative evidence of the difficulties a user has working a product, prototype or simulation.

In the last section we argued that prototypes and simulations should be considered as user interface specifications. The point of developing any form of specification, rather than diving straight into implementation, is that a specification is relatively easy to change, whereas an implementation is not. The first requirement on a technique for testing and improving a user interface then is that it can be applied early on before there is a full working system. Design tends to be 'opportunistic'. You might specify some part of the interface rather broadly and then another in quite some detail, returning to specify the former in more detail later on. To fit this natural opportunistic style, a technique for testing a user interface specification should be applicable to partial designs. Opportunistic design is a natural way of working as the way one develops one part of the interface helps to constrain the form of other parts. This means that an evaluation technique needs to be applied to each part as it is developed, not at the end when the design is complete.

Cooperative Evaluation can be applied to partial prototypes and simulations. Also since the designer set the tasks for the user to do it is possible to control what part of the system is tested and to steer the user away from parts of the system that do not yet exist. Our first requirement of a technique for testing the usability of a user interface was that it should not require a full working system. That is, it should be applicable with any of the prototypes or simulations described above. The next requirement is that it should be applicable rapidly.

As explained in the last section, Cooperative Evaluation is designed to be used in the early stages of design when the specification is changing rapidly. This means that to be useful the technique must be applicable rapidly. One implication of this requirement is that designers should evaluate their own designs. The alternative is for the designers to explain their design to an evaluator who then has to communicate back the results of the testing. This process of communication can take as much time as the testing itself and so a technique that can be used by the designers themselves has a considerable advantage over one that requires a human factors expert to apply it. Software designers have a variety of skills but they are unlikely to have much knowledge of human factors. So, if an evaluation technique is to be used by designers, it must also be easily learned.

Finally, the user interface is being tested in order to improve it. This gives rise to a third requirement, that is, that the testing method should give rise to appropriate feedback. Some evaluation techniques only provide rather global measures of how good or bad an interface is. This may be appropriate for quality assurance at the end of the design process, but it is of little help to the designer wanting to know what changes to make to improve an early prototype. What is required at this stage is detailed feedback concerning what features cause what problems.

Cooperative Evaluation meets these three requirements. It does not need a full working system. It can be applied rapidly and it provides feedback in a form that designers can understand and use. The next section describes how this is achieved.

1.7 How does Cooperative Evaluation work?

Synopsis

Q. What is Cooperative Evaluation?

A. Representative users work through representative tasks chosen by the designer.

As they work they explain to the designer what they are doing and ask questions.

The designer allows the user to make mistakes and uses the user's questions to elicit further information about a potential problem.

Unexpected behaviour and comments about the interface are viewed as symptoms of potential usability problems.

Chapter 2 provides a step-by-step procedure for testing a user interface using Cooperative Evaluation. First, the target user population is defined and representative users recruited. Next, tasks are constructed for the users to carry out with the prototype. These are designed to exercise the relevant parts of the prototype.

Prior to the testing session it is explained that it is the prototype that is being tested not the user. The user is encouraged to think aloud while working through the tasks and if not the designer prompts the user to do so, e.g. 'What has the system done now?', 'What do you want to do?' The designer allows the user to make mistakes and does not always answer the user's request for help directly. In this way the user provides empirical evidence of what problems any user might have trying to learn and use the system on their own.

Throughout this process the designer is looking for two kinds of evidence that there may be a problem with the prototype user interface: unexpected behaviour and comments about the interface. These are theoretically based concepts that depend on a particular model of human−computer interaction.

Figure 1.6 depicts one view or model of how people interact with a computer. The user has some goals or intentions, for example, changing the mistyped word 'geat' to 'great'. These goals have to be translated into actions such as keystrokes or mouse clicks. The system translates these actions into effects some of which will be visible to the user via the display. The user evaluates these effects and modifies the goals accordingly. This model is the basis of a number of theories in cognitive psychology and has been used to provide successful computational models of how people perform this kind of task. Our interest in this viewpoint is that it defines the information necessary to detect a particular kind of problem users may have.

Unexpected behaviour is detected when the evaluator's knowledge of the user's goals suggests a different action to that which the user actually takes. In many cases the designer will think of unexpected behaviour as an 'error'. For example, the designer knows that it is possible to insert a letter, 'r' into 'great', and expects the user to complete the task this way but the user insists on retyping the whole word. It is necessary to get the users to think aloud as they work in order to find out what their current goal is. If one does not know what they are trying to achieve, there is no way of knowing if they are going about it as expected.

Having users think aloud as they work is also crucial to the detection of the other symptom of a potential problem with a user interface, comments on the interface. While Figure 1.6 may be an adequate model of the information exchanged in human−computer interaction it does not, normally, correspond to the user's subjective experience. If the user interface is working well it should not enter the user's awareness. This is illustrated in Figure 1.7. The user concentrates on the goal and the current state, e.g. the user is aware that a word is currently spelt 'geat' and it should be 'great'. Without thinking about the actions to be taken, they are just done. This idea that a good tool should be 'transparent' is due to Heidegger. He uses the example of a hammer. In normal use one is aware of a goal (getting a nail flush with the surface) and the current state (it sticks up 1 cm). One does not think about the height the hammer has to be raised or the force to be applied, one simply hammers.

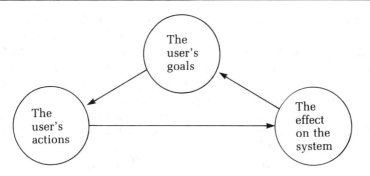

Figure 1.6
A model of human–
computer interaction

Occasionally there will be a breakdown, perhaps the hammer is too small for the job, perhaps the head is loose. In Heidegger's terms, this physical breakdown is accompanied by a breakdown in the user's experience. They will suddenly need to think in more detail about the actions they are taking.

A breakdown then corresponds to the user being aware of the full process, as depicted in Figure 1.6, rather than just the goal and current state as in Figure 1.7. Such 'breakdowns' are apparent in what the user says while thinking aloud. When the user interface is working well, their comments will all be at the task level (e.g. 'I want to insert an "r" here'). A comment about the user interface indicates that all is not well (e.g. 'I find it very difficult to find the insertion cursor'). Sometimes unexpected behaviour will be accompanied by a comment on the user interface but it is also possible for unexpected behaviour to occur without comments and comments without unexpected behaviour. An important example of the latter is where a user is doing the task exactly in the way the designer had intended but finds it very awkward or tedious. Readers who are interested in the nature of unexpected behaviour and comments may like to read the paper by Wright and Monk (1989) mentioned in the Bibliography.

In the above discussion we have been careful to refer to unexpected behaviour and comments as symptoms of potential problems in the prototype user interface. They are only potential problems because some of the difficulties a user has may be trivial. The designer has to exercise some judgement here.

Figure 1.7
Transparency of tool
use

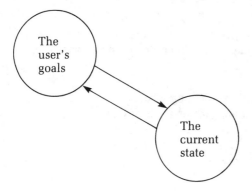

Our experience is that this is much easier than one would expect. The important deficiencies of the prototype are obvious, *once they have been pointed out* in this way. What is much more difficult is to understand what the underlying problem really is. For this reason it is best to view unexpected behaviour and comments as symptoms and not always to take the user's behaviour and comments at face value. For example, one might take the comment 'I find it very difficult to find the insertion cursor' as a plea for a bigger and more obvious cursor. A deeper analysis might question why the user is looking for it in the first place.

In summary, the characteristics of Cooperative Evaluation are:

1. Users work through tasks selected by the designer.
2. Users work with a prototype or simulation.
3. Users think aloud and ask questions while working and the designer may similarly ask the user questions.
4. The designer looks for unexpected behaviour and comments on the user interface from the user.

These characteristics come from our analysis of the requirements of a technique for testing a user interface specification (see the section 'What is required?'). The first characteristic, that tasks have to be selected by the designer, follows from the requirement that 'It should not need a full working system'. The alternative would be to allow free use ('use this in your day-to-day work') which is not possible with a partial prototype. A user must be guided to the relevant part of the prototype and prevented from attempting to do things that the prototype cannot support. Characteristics 2 and 3 follow from the requirements that 'it should be applicable rapidly' and 'natural to users and designers alike'. Chapters 3 and 4 present some evidence that this is indeed the case. Finally, characteristic 4 follows from the requirement that 'It should provide the maximum feedback about how the design should be changed, that is, it should provide detailed qualitative evidence of the difficulties a user has working a product, prototype or simulation.'

1.8   Other techniques

Synopsis

Q. What other techniques are likely to be most useful?

A. Four are discussed

1. Techniques that do something else:
    For requirements analysis and job design
        Contextual Enquiry
    For quality assurance
        Usability Engineering

2. Techniques to do the same job but do not involve users:
    Cognitive Walkthrough
    Heuristic Evaluation

The 'niche' occupied by Cooperative Evaluation as a testing technique is limited by the characteristics described in the last section. These are

(a) that the designer chooses the tasks the user will do and
(b) that the user thinks aloud.

At the very earliest stages of design the problem is to understand the work the user is doing and what tasks the system should support. Having the designer select tasks makes Cooperative Evaluation suitable for use with an early partial prototype but unsuitable for this kind of requirements analysis. At the end of the design process there may be a need for some kind of quantitative measure of usability. Having the users think aloud is necessary to provide the rich feedback needed to improve a specification but makes quantitative measures not representative of real performance. The former problem, understanding the tasks to support, can be facilitated by a technique known as 'Contextual Enquiry', the latter problem, of measuring usability, by a technique called 'Usability Engineering'. These techniques are both described in some detail in a paper by Whiteside, Bennett and Holtzblatt (1988). Their essential characteristics are described in Figures 1.8 and 1.9.

In Contextual Enquiry users are observed and interviewed at their place of work. The technique has its origins in anthropology. It focuses on the experiences of users as they work and the objective is to see the work through

Procedure

1. Users are interviewed in the work place to explore the nature of their work.

2. 'A period of observation and interpretation follows during which the usability engineer observes and questions the user while the user describes what he or she is doing. Together the user and usability engineer interpret the user's experience of the computer system.' (p. 34)

Figure 1.8
Contextual Enquiry
(Whiteside, Bennett
and Holtzblatt, 1987).
This method focuses
on the user's
experience in the
work context

Usability requirement: Installability
Target users: secretaries and similar office personnel

Worst case	Planned level	Best case	Now level
1 day	1 hour	10 mins	Many can't install

Figure 1.9
Usability Engineering
(Whiteside, Bennett
and Holtzblatt, 1987).
An example of
usability requirement.
This technique
depends on
quantitative measures

the eyes of the user and to free oneself from conclusions based on one's own perspective. To do this effectively and efficiently requires considerable training and experience, and this may be a technique that is best reserved for specialists.

Usability Engineering involves setting usability requirements. Then, towards the end of system development, the system can be tested to see whether these requirements have been met. This is strictly analogous to the process of setting system performance requirements (e.g. 'the worst case seek time for this disk drive will be 100 ms'). Usability requirements provide a 'stopping rule', i.e. a way of deciding when it is time to stop trying to further improve the user interface. They may also play an important part in quality assurance. Extracting quantitative measures from people requires a certain amount of expertise if the measures obtained are to be representative and this may be another technique for the specialist. Having designers assess their own systems at this stage would be questionable anyway.

Usability Engineering and Contextual Enquiry are techniques designed to do quite different jobs to Cooperative Evaluation. The next two techniques to be considered here are, like Cooperative Evaluation, intended to be used by designers to improve their prototype user interface specifications. Cognitive Walkthrough is an analysis of the cognitive processing required to use an interface; while Heuristic Evaluation involves evaluating the prototype against a set of guidelines. Neither involves users in the process. They are characterised in Figures 1.10 and 1.11 respectively.

Cognitive Walkthrough was originally devised for use with very simple user interfaces such as the walk-up-and-use interfaces found in public exhibitions and stores. Here the user's goals are straightforward (e.g. 'find the location of the hardware department'). With more complex tasks, goals have to be decomposed before they can be acted upon. Figure 1.12 outlines a hypothetical goal structure for editing a manuscript. Goal 1.1 is not achieved until its subgoals have been achieved (1.1.1, 1.1.2 and 1.1.3). Similarly, Goal 1 is not achieved until all its subgoals (1.1, 1.2 and so on) have been achieved. Figure 1.12 only specifies the top level goal structure for editing a document. For example, Goal 1.1.3 has to be further decomposed before the actions that have to be taken can be specified.

Step 1 in Figure 1.10 involves describing the top level goals for the task. Step 2 is to describe how the system works from the point of view of the user. That is, what actions users can take and the visible effect they have

Figure 1.10
Cognitive
Walkthrough
(Rieman *et al.*, 1991)

Procedure

1. The designer describes a hypothetical user's task.

2. The designer specifies the actions to be taken to complete the task and the effect each action has on the display.

3. The designer answers questions about the user's supposed goals and sub-goals and how these map onto the actions required and the changes in the display.

Procedure

The designer goes through the design evaluating it against the following heuristics:

Use a simple and natural dialogue
Provide an intuitive visual layout
Speak the user's language
Minimise the user's memory load
Be consistent
Provide feedback
Provide clearly marked exits
Provide shortcuts
Provide good help
Allow user customisation
Minimise the use and effects of modes
Support input device continuity

Figure 1.11
Heuristic Evaluation (Nielsen and Molich, 1990). This list is a modified version of the original; by Karat, Campbell and Fiegel (1992) (see Bibliography)

on the system. Step 3 is to describe how the user gets from the top level goals to taking the correct actions by elaborating the goal structure. While doing this the designer is required to make judgements such as whether the display will prompt the right sub-goals in the user's mind. The whole procedure is administered using forms. The authors of this technique suggest that it might be used by a group of designers in peer review procedures in the same way that code walkthroughs are used in many organisations. For simple user interfaces, Cognitive Walkthrough may be a useful precursor to Cooperative Evaluation. As such it could remove some initial problems and will serve to focus design on the user's task so that the prototype tested with real users is as good as possible. With more complex interfaces it is questionable whether the technique could be used by designers without considerable help from human factors specialists.

Nielsen and Molich (1990) have proposed a technique they call 'Heuristic Evaluation'. Here the designer applies a number of principles or heuristics to the prototype design. They present data to back up their claim that designers can use this technique effectively with minimal training. Again, this would seem to be a good technique to use prior to Cooperative Evaluation to ensure that the prototype tested with real users is as good as possible.

Researchers are now beginning to compare the effectiveness of different techniques in experiments. Typically these experiments involve having different

Goal 1: edit manuscript
    Goal 1.1: edit first error
        Goal 1.1.1: find next error on paper
        Goal 1.1.2: find next error on screen
        Goal 1.1.3: move cursor and edit
    Goal 1.2: edit next error

Figure 1.12
Part of the hypothetical goal structure for editing a document

people use different methods to assess the same user interface. Effectiveness is assessed as the average number of problems detected using the different methods to be compared. They may also compute the average amount of time spent doing each evaluation to give an estimate of cost as well. Two such experiments are cited in the Bibliography (Jeffries *et al.*, 1991; and Karat, Campbell and Fiegel, 1992). Neither used the designers of the system evaluated as evaluators and their findings cannot be used to make judgements about the relative cost-effectiveness of Cooperative Evaluation by designers versus Heuristic Evaluation or Cognitive Walkthrough. There is obviously a need for experiments that do allow us to compare these three techniques. In Chapter 4 we present two experiments of our own. These do not compare Cooperative Evaluation with other techniques but they do serve to validate some of our claims about its cost effectiveness.

In summary, four techniques that may be considered complementary to Cooperative Evaluation have been described. Two have quite different purposes to Cooperative Evaluation. Contextual Enquiry is for use in the early stages of requirement definition. Usability Engineering is for use in the final stages of design and quality assurance. Two have the same aims as Cooperative Evaluation; that is they are for use by designers to improve a partial prototype. We suggest that Cognitive Walkthough and Heuristic Evaluation are used prior to applying Cooperative Evaluation. Using more than one technique should maximise the number of potential problems detected.

1.9   Concluding comments — Cooperative Evaluation as Participatory Design

In this chapter we have explained why there is a need for techniques such as Cooperative Evaluation and why Cooperative Evaluation takes the form that it does. We have also discussed some other techniques that may be used for the same or related purposes. These were selected as the most potentially useful of the techniques available.

The chapter has focused on the task of detecting problems in a user interface specification. However, this is only one of the ways in which using Cooperative Evaluation can improve the final design. The other is by making the designer more aware of the user's point of view. The benefits of bringing designers and users together in a non-threatening situation such as a Cooperative Evaluation session cannot be over-estimated. Both come to understand the constraints under which the other operates, designers come to understand why the users find certain things difficult and the users why designers cannot always do exactly what they want them to. In this sense Cooperative Evaluation can be seen as a technique for Participatory Design, that is, a way of getting users and designers to communicate effectively about the design. For management there is also the important side effect of enhancing the company's quality assurance techniques. Cognitive Walkthrough and Heuristic Evaluation cannot serve this purpose as they do not involve users.

2 Cooperative Evaluation: how to do it

2.1 Topics covered in this chapter

- A short introduction to Cooperative Evaluation
- Recruit users
- Prepare tasks
- Interact and record
- Summarise your observations

2.1.1 How to use this chapter

This chapter is a 'how to' guide. It provides a framework for managing evaluations, guidelines for planning and running them, and advice on countering problems which may occur within a session. Finally, there is some advice about how to use the results of the evaluation.

Appendix 1 is an abridged version of this chapter with checklists substituted for much of the text. You are advised to read this chapter first and then, when you have some understanding of what is required, to use Appendix 1 to run evaluation sessions.

2.2 Introduction

2.2.1 What is Cooperative Evaluation?

As was explained in Chapter 1, Cooperative Evaluation is a procedure for obtaining data about problems experienced when working with a prototype for a software product, so that changes can be made to improve it. What makes Cooperative Evaluation distinctive is the collaboration that occurs as users and designers evaluate the system together. Users are encouraged to ask the evaluator questions about interacting with the system and the evaluator asks them questions about their understanding of the system. This makes the procedure seem very natural to the users and requires fewer resources than more formal testing methods.

2.2.2 Who uses Cooperative Evaluation?

Cooperative evaluation is primarily intended for use by designers without specialised knowledge of human factors research. It can, however, be used with equal effectiveness by human factors specialists requiring quick and easy to obtain feedback about systems they have been asked to evaluate.

2.2.3 When to use Cooperative Evaluation

The forms that prototypes can take and where Cooperative Evaluation sits in the design process are discussed in some detail in Chapter 1. Cooperative Evaluation is most useful for early feedback for redesign in a rapid iterative cycle. The aim is not to provide an exhaustive list of all the problems that could possibly be identified. Rather, it is to help you identify the most important improvements to consider with the minimum of effort. Cooperative Evaluation can be used with:

- an existing product that is to be improved or extended;
- an early partial prototype or simulation;
- a full working prototype.

In Cooperative Evaluation users work through a set of tasks with the system. For this reason it is not suitable for the earliest stages of systems analysis when such tasks have yet to be determined. Also, because users and evaluator work cooperatively, and because the evaluator is the designer, the method is not suitable for quality assurance settings. Quality assurance usually requires that the assessment be carried out by a disinterested third party.

2.2.4 Steps to be taken

What follows is a step-by-step procedure for Cooperative Evaluation. The essential features of the method are as follows:

(a) Recruit users: You recruit one or more users to help in the evaluation. They are chosen to be, in some sense, typical of the population of people who will eventually use the system. If several users are to take part, they should be chosen to reflect the range of skills, aptitudes and personalities of the eventual end users.

(b) Prepare tasks: You specify a set of tasks for the users. These are chosen in order to allow the users to explore those areas of the system that will be relevant to their work. In the case of early partial simulations they also serve to limit users' exploration to the functions currently available.

(c) Interact and record: Each user works with the system and you note the problems they have. The procedure is designed to help them to verbalise the problems they experience through thinking aloud. What they say and do is recorded and notes are made.

(d) Summarise your observations: Using your notes about where the user had problems, you can go back to the recording of the session to re-examine precisely what the problem was and how it might be fixed.

2.3   Recruit users

2.3.1   Define the target user population

Before you can say whether someone is typical or atypical of the eventual users of the product you have to define who those eventual users will be. This step is to give a name to and write down the target user population. Examples are: 'junior office personnel', 'level 3 managers in the purchasing department', 'naval ratings'.

1. If the product is to be used by a specified department or group of individuals then the existing employees define this population. This would be the case if you are designing an interface to a 'bespoke' system. In such a case it may even be possible to name the individuals who are going to be your users!
2. It may be more difficult to know who are the users of a generic product being developed for a large market. However, in this case the project is likely to have been preceded by market research which may be able to supply some of the relevant facts. Even if the population is not defined for you it is a good idea to make an explicit decision to aim at some target user population. If you do not there is always the danger that different members of the design team will be implicitly designing for different people. Without precise definition, designers design for people like themselves. This is potentially disastrous as the eventual users are often very different.

2.3.2   Recruit users who are as similar to the target user population as is practical

1. Decide how many users it is practicable to test. You will have to estimate how much time you need with each user (see the section 'Prepare Tasks' below). In our experience, even working with one user can provide a lot of useful information. Additional users will help identify the recurrent problems and make the evaluation more complete. If you can work with more than one user choose people who represent the whole range of your target user population. That is, choose people who are as different as possible, rather than similar, within this population. The question of how many users to work with is discussed in Chapter 4, where it is concluded that five is probably the maximum. If you have the resources for more it is better to use the feedback provided by the first five to change the prototype and then to evaluate the next iteration with the additional users.
2. It will often be possible to recruit people directly from the population

you decide on. The advantage of this is that they will more readily 'buy in' to the new system. They will feel, correctly, that they had a hand in its development and so have a stake in its ownership. The danger of working with people who will be the eventual users of the product is that this feeling of ownership will develop too fast. You may then meet opposition when you want to change and improve the prototype. To avoid this it is important to stress the provisional form of the ideas you are trying out. For this reason 'rough and ready' prototypes such as paper simulations are often to be preferred to more polished looking simulations using software.

3. If you cannot recruit people directly from the target user population you should attempt to find people with the same characteristics, such as:
    • their knowledge of the task domain;
    • their experience with other computer systems;
    • their skill at using the keyboard and other input devices;
    • their level of education and how they will approach situations which require problem solving.

To what extent you can recruit typical users will depend largely on practical constraints, but testing less than ideal users is better than no testing. Research workers often use the following groups to approximate to a particular target user population:

• Members of the general public recruited by newspaper advertisements
• Students
• Workers with specific skills recruited from temporary employment agencies

At this stage there are also a number of practical details that have to be taken care of. You may need to make arrangements to pay users, to have someone cover for them and so on.

Finally, do not under-estimate the amount of time it will take you to recruit suitable users for Cooperative Evaluation. Arranging for someone to come to an evaluation session can often take nearly as long as the session itself.

2.4   Prepare tasks

Cooperative Evaluation depends on the users having some tasks to do. These should be reasonably specific, e.g. 'edit the instructions for this lathe so that they . . .', rather than very general, e.g. 'do your normal work'. Selecting the right tasks for the user to do is crucial to the success of the technique.

First of all the tasks must be representative of the work that the product will support. This will not be possible unless you have a good understanding of what that work involves. Cooperative Evaluation assumes that the ground work necessary for this has already been done. Chapter 1 gives references to a technique known as Contextual Enquiry that is designed to help derive such a model of the user's tasks. Secondly, they should limit the user to the part of the system that you are setting out to evaluate. This should be reasonably well focused. Choosing fairly specific tasks will keep the user to this focus. Very general tasks may lead the user to try functions that you cannot simulate in the current prototype or that you are not interested in at that moment.

The tasks chosen have to fit the following constraints:

- They should be suitable to the stage of design that you are evaluating. When rapid prototyping with a partial mock-up or simulation, the nature of the simulation may well limit the tasks considered. With a full working system you can use a mixture of specific and slightly more general tasks.
- They should be practical within the time allowed. In general, something useful can be achieved in between one and ten hours. When evaluating a prototype, time has to be allowed for the users to learn the new system. With large systems it may only be possible to evaluate core functions or fragments of the user interface. Decide on the maximum time you can spend with each user and then plan your tasks to fit that time. If there is a lot to learn it is probably better to work with two users for ten hours each than four users for five hours each.
- The set of tasks should ensure that the user examines the parts of the system they will use in their daily work with the final product. For this reason, every effort should be made to understand the work of the target user population before such tasks are specified. Important functions should be examined twice, once at the beginning and once at the end of the session. At the beginning you may observe problems in learning these functions and, at the end, more persistent problems. Important functions should also be evaluated in a variety of task contexts.
- They should be expressed in terms the users will understand.

Again, do not under-estimate the time it will take to set up a Cooperative Evaluation session. Selecting tasks and getting the prototype into a suitable form will probably take several times longer than the session. As a rule of thumb, allow five times the length of the testing session for this preparation, e.g. five hours for a one-hour testing session. But remember, the five hours is a constant irrespective of the number of users you work with.

The steps to be taken are as follows.

2.4.1 Write the task instructions for the user

Write down the tasks in a form suitable for presentation to the users. This document will be referred to as the 'task sheet'. Make sure that the tasks are written in terms of work or 'business' goals rather than functions of the system. In the context of a word processor, 'access the *replace* function' is a bad task as it presumes knowledge of the system. 'Change *geat* to *great*' is a good task because it is specified in terms of the user's goals and independently of the functions provided.

2.4.2   Estimate the time it will take to complete each task

This will probably involve working through the tasks yourself. Allow for the time it takes to introduce the users to the system and the time they will spend explaining their experiences. You will almost certainly under-estimate the time required. Avoid any tendency to rush the users through the tasks and make sure that the most important functions are examined early in the session and again later.

Check that it will still be possible to work with the number of users decided on in 'Recruit Users'. It may be necessary to adjust the tasks set at this stage to fit in with practical constraints.

2.4.3   Try out the instructions and task sheet

It is useful to have a dry run of the session with a friend or colleague. This need not be a full blown Cooperative Evaluation session. Rather the aim is to check that the instructions and task sheet will be understandable to the user.

2.5   Interact and record

This section describes how to run the session itself. It is divided into five sub-sections: 'Before the users arrive' allows you to check that you have everything ready; 'When the users arrive' describes how to put the users at ease and explain what is required of them. This is probably the most difficult part of running a session. Users will often come expecting that their competence is to be tested, not the effectiveness of the prototype. You and the user may each have a different status in the organisation; at the very least you will probably not have met before. All these factors make for a poor exchange of information, so it is very important to establish a good working relationship before you start. 'While the users are using the system' describes what to look for as the session progresses, what to record and how to keep the user talking. 'What to do if . . . Some hints to help you through the session' is for trouble shooting. Finally, 'Debriefing' describes what to do at the end of the session when the user has finished the set tasks.

2.5.1   Before the users arrive

You will need:

- Your prototype ready to use in a reasonably quiet environment
- A sheet containing the tasks for the users to carry out (the task sheet, see above)
- Some way of recording what the users say (see below)
- Some way of recording what they do (see below)
- A notebook or form for recording problems as they arise

- A list of questions to ask at the end of the session (see the sub-section 'Debriefing')

There are various ways of recording how the user interacts with the prototype. The best record is obtained by 'instrumenting' a software prototype. This means adding to the software procedures that create a file that records a transcript of the user's actions and the effects this has on the prototype. Such a record is known as a system log (an example of such a log is given as Figure 4.3 in Chapter 4). There are also software products available for making demonstrations as 'movies' of system usage. These can be used to make a record of the session, though they tend to be very expensive on disk space. An alternative is to make a video recording with the camera pointing at the screen. This has the advantage that the audio record of what the user says is synchronised with the system log, however, it is much more intrusive and may put off some users. A video camera placed above the table you are working on is a good way of recording interaction with a paper prototype. If these alternatives are not available, you can do quite well by having a colleague sit behind you and take notes on what happens. Alternatively, use a cassette recorder to obtain a record of what the user says and take notes of what they do. Working only from an audio tape will still yield useful information.

The best recordings of what the user says are obtained with a clip on microphone. Attach this to the user's clothing as near to their mouth as possible. A separate microphone for the evaluator/designer will only be necessary in extreme circumstances as it is less important that your part of the conversation is recorded clearly.

Before you start:

1. Check you have everything in the bulleted list above.
2. Work through all the tasks on the task sheet. This will serve to check there are no bugs in your procedure. Also it will serve to familiarise you with how the system supports the tasks the users will attempt.
3. Check out the quality of the audio and video recording before you start. In particular the audio microphone should be placed carefully so as to avoid background noise from disk drives and so on.
4. If you are using a cassette recorder reset the tape counter.

2.5.2   When the users arrive

Spend some time creating an informal *cooperative* atmosphere. Put the users at their ease. The whole session should be conducted in an informal manner and you and the users should discuss the system openly. They should be encouraged to think of themselves as coevaluators not as experimental subjects. They should be told that you are interested in the way the system misleads them rather than in the mistakes they make. They should be told you are interested in the things that the system makes it hard for them to do rather than the things that they are unable to do. This emphasises that it is the system that is being evaluated not the user. This will help the question–answer dialogue to flow easily. You should, however, keep control of the situation and make sure that the dialogue does not drift off the point, which is getting information about this particular system as used by the particular user.

The users should only be given the minimum information they need about how to use the system. The aim is to get them to find out how to use it by interacting with it and with you. You still need to explain what Cooperative Evaluation involves and to introduce the task sheet. Cooperative Evaluation is best explained orally, rather than giving the users an instruction sheet, but we include an instruction sheet as Figure 2.1 to give you an idea of what such an explanation might sound like.

So, when the user arrives:

1. Put the user at ease. Remind them that it is the system that is being tested.
2. Start recording the session.
3. Introduce yourself by name and describe what the session is about in general terms.
4. Describe the technique of Cooperative Evaluation.
5. Introduce the task sheet to the user to give a general idea of what they will be doing.

2.5.3   While the users are using the system

1. Note each occurrence of unexpected behaviour and each comment on the usability of the system (see the section 'Summarise your observations' for further explanation of what is required). If there are two evaluators present one of you should decide to be the chief interactant while the other one takes notes. If there is only one evaluator then it will only be possible to make very brief notes about important points; the rest will have to be committed to memory. Notes can contain cross-references to places in the tape. Write down the reading on the tape counter of a cassette recorder or note the time since the session began for a video recording. These specific points on the recording can then be followed up to jog your memory later without you having to re-examine it all. Try not to let note taking interfere with the primary task of creating a dialogue with the user.
2. Encourage the users to think aloud while using the system. This can be achieved by asking them to give you a running commentary of what they are doing and what's going on, or simply by asking them to tell you what they are thinking.
3. Ensure that there is a relatively continuous dialogue by asking appropriate open questions whenever possible. Non-verbal communication can be useful here. Nods, smiles and a carefully timed 'mm mm' all help.

Thank you for agreeing to help with this study. Today we are going to evaluate the usability of a particular computer system called Mind Bender.

Mind Bender stores large numbers of references to academic works rather like the catalogues in a library. It can be used to search for things written on a particular subject, or by a particular author and so on.

The aim of the study is to find out how easy Mind Bender is to use by people like yourself. We want you to use it to help us find out what problems Mind Bender poses and how it could be improved.

We will give you some standard tasks to do using Mind Bender. The aim of this is to allow us to get some information about how Mind Bender supports this activity. We're particularly interested in situations in which Mind Bender encourages you to make errors in selecting commands and misleads you about what it will do. We are also interested in extra commands that would make the system easier to use.

To get this information we shall use a question-and-answer technique. This involves three things.

1. We want you to think-out-loud as you do each task telling us how you are trying to solve each task, which commands you think might be appropriate and why, and what you think the machine has done in response to your commands and why. Think of this as you giving us a running commentary on what you are doing and thinking.

2. Whenever you find yourself in a situation where you are unsure about what to do or what effect commands might have, ask us for advice. If you ask us what you need to know we will suggest things for you to try but if you get really stuck we'll explain exactly what you have to do.

3. In addition we will ask you questions about what you are trying to do and what effect you expect the commands you type will have. This is simply to find out what problems there are with the system. During our conversations, we want you to voice any thoughts you have about parts of the system which you feel are difficult to use or poorly designed.

While you're doing this we'll be noting down the problems you mention but in case we miss any we are going to audio tape our conversation. This recording will be anonymous and treated in confidence.

Remember it's not you we're testing, it's Mind Bender. We are interested in what you think so don't treat this as an examination. Treat it as a structured discussion about Mind Bender. Please feel free to say whatever you think about the system and the tasks you're given to solve.

Figure 2.1
Sample instructions for explaining Cooperative Evaluation

The following questions will generally give the information you require:

- How do we do that?
- What do you want to do?
- What will happen if . . .?
- What has the system done now?
- What is the system trying to tell you with this message?
- Why has the system done that?
- What were you expecting to happen then?

For example:

1. After the users read each task (get them to read it out aloud) ask them: 'How do we do that?' This will yield information about their intentions.
2. As the users consider an item in a menu ask them: 'What will happen if you choose that item?'
3. When the users have entered a command and the system has responded ask them: 'What has the system done?' or 'What is the information on that part of the screen telling you?' This can be followed up by asking the users 'Why has the system done that?', or if they appear confused or surprised ask them, 'What were you expecting to happen?' Finding out about things that did not happen that the users expected would happen is very informative.

The users must be allowed to make mistakes, find problems, and ask you questions. These are your data, so do not anticipate mistakes and correct them before they are made. Do not tell the users what problems they are having, let them tell you. When they have made a mistake or asked you a question consider whether you want to find out more before answering them. So, for example, if a user asks you 'Should I press return when I've entered the data line?' you may feel that this is a relatively simple query and that you are not too interested in pursuing the matter further, so you may simply answer 'Yes'. If, on the other hand, the user says 'What does the DISPLAY command do?' you might want to pursue this further by asking the user to hazard a guess as to what it might do. By doing this you might get some information about possible misconceptions about the meaning of the command. If, of course, after several guesses the user has still not come up with the right answer you will tell them what the command does but you will have learned quite a bit along the way. You must also ask the user questions when they do something unexpected or say something that does not make sense to you. Be careful, however, not to appear too critical. For example, it is not necessarily a good idea to say, 'Why did you do that?' as this can put users on the defensive. Instead you might ask them, 'What were you expecting the system to do when you did that?' Figure 2.2 is a transcript of a Cooperative Evaluation session to illustrate this kind of question and answer dialogue. It should be read in conjunction with Figure 2.3 which contains comments on what happened.

Immediately after testing you will probably find that you have noticed many

Figure 2.2
Extract from a
Cooperative
Evaluation session

The following is a transcript taken from a study of a novice user of a bibliographic database tool. It is intended to give you a flavour of how a Cooperative Evaluation session should go. The user is attempting a search operation which is carried out by selecting the initial letter of the commands. Quotation marks indicate that the user is reading directly from the screen or the task sheet. Comments on the user's behaviour are in bold.

The user reads her task:

1. User: Okay 'find the title of the paper by Thomas and
2. Gould 1974'. So I press S for select. 'Type initial letter'
3. So I press T for Thomas — no I don't I type N for name of
4. author which is Thomas and Gould.
5. **The user types in 'Thomas and Gould' but the**
6. **system only accepts one author name at a**
7. **time.**
8. User: Do I need to press return?
9. Eval: Yes. Press return and it will carry out the
10. command.
11. **The system searches database returns no**
12. **selection and displays the main menu.**
13. Eval: Okay what do you think the system has done
14. now?
15. User: Well it's looked for the reference so I now
16. guess I have to press D for display to find the title.
17. **This won't work because nothing has been**
18. **selected.**
19. Eval: Okay try that.
20. **The user presses D. Nothing happens.**
21. User: Nothing's happened.
22. Eval: Why do you think that might be?
23. User: I don't know.
24. **The evaluator points to the selection box**
25. **which indicates no selection was made.**
26. Eval: What do you think this window tells you?
27. User: Oh, I didn't see that box, it hasn't found the
28. reference.

problems and have several comments to make which you have not had time to note down during the session. It is a good idea to consolidate these immediately after the session while they are fresh in your mind. This can either be done in discussion with your colleague, or if you are testing alone by making some more detailed notes. Alternatively, they can be dictated on to the recording.

2.5.4 What to do if . . . Some hints to help you through the session

While all of what you have read so far might sound quite straightforward there are a number of problems that you may run into. These problems are discussed below.

Figure 2.3
Some points about
the transcript
example in Figure 2.2

Lines 1—2 Here the evaluator has got the user to read out the task. This helps the evaluator when the tape is analysed and helps the user to become relaxed with the audio taping.

Lines 2—4 Here the user indicates that she has understood that the way to select the search option from the main menu is by typing the first letter. But in the subsidiary menu requiring the user to specify what field she wishes to search by she interprets the menu prompt 'type initial letter' as referring to the author she wishes to find rather than the field she wishes to search for. She does in fact correct herself before inputting anything. It is nevertheless indicative of a potential problem for other users. The evaluator, because the user corrects herself, decides not to pick up on this.

Lines 5—7 These comments inform the reader what the user has done. These could be obtained from a system log after the session or noted at the time.

They also indicate that the user has made a mistake because the system only accepts one author at a time. This kind of mistake is referred to as unexpected behavour (see 'Summarise your observations' below).

Lines 8—10 The user asks a straightforward question and the evaluator makes a decision to answer it directly because he is not too interested in the user learning when to press returns. But note, he might have made a different decision if the system being evaluated had been a text editor where the return key has a much more central role to play.

Lines 11—14 Indicate what the system did in response to the input. It returned no selection because it treated the two author names as a single name. Thus the user's initial mistake has led to an inappropriate response from the system. Rather than tell the user what has gone wrong, the evaluator decides to pursue the problem further by asking the user for the interpretation of the system's response.

Lines 15—18 The user's response to the question indicates that she has failed to notice that nothing has been selected. This suggests to the evaluator that the window providing feedback about the outcome of a search might not be salient enough for novice users.

Lines 19—22 The evaluator holds off from explaining the problem to the user and instead encourages the user to follow through her own line of enquiry. By doing this the user finds out for herself that something has gone wrong. The evaluator still holds off from explaining the problem encouraging the user to think diagnostically about the problem.

Lines 23—28 But the user is stuck for ideas so the evaluator shows her the box indicating that nothing has been selected. In response the user confirms the evaluator's belief that she had failed to notice this information, but that when it is pointed out to her she understands clearly what information it provides. The dialogue goes on from here with the user working out (eventually) where she went wrong.

The shy or reticent user

Some users may be shy about the recording or worried about making a fool of themselves. They may be reluctant to ask you questions for fear of appearing ignorant. They may also be worried about confidentiality. You must do all you can to put them at their ease by emphasising that the recording is only for your own use and no one else will hear it, and that it is the system and not the user that is being tested. You must tell them that it is important for them to ask questions even though they may appear trivial, as other people may not find them so trivial.

The absorbed user

As the users get more and more absorbed in carrying out the tasks they have been given to do they may forget about talking to you and you will feel disinclined to interrupt them. At these times you must get them talking again by asking them relevant questions or paraphrasing what you think they are doing at the moment.

The inarticulate user

You may have problems with a user who is inarticulate, saying things that you don't understand or using too many 'it's', 'that's' and other pronouns so that you do not know what they are referring to. At these times you must prompt the user to explain what they mean.

The disinterested or defensive user

The users may not come to you with an open mind about what they will be doing and whether it will be interesting. In your initial introduction you must make every effort to get the user interested in the study, emphasising the value of the work in terms of wanting to make computers more usable and (when relevant) that it will have direct impact on their work practices. Most people, if they are primed correctly, find it quite interesting to think about how they think and the way in which they can be misled by bad interfaces. The Cooperative Evaluation method should be introduced as an interesting and natural way of 'thinking about thinking' and 'thinking about interfaces'. Getting the user interested in participating in the study will depend on presenting yourself as interested and taking the job seriously (but without becoming too officious).

The intimidated user

You must remember that in carrying out this study you are asking someone who may be unsophisticated in the use of computers to come along and carry out quite difficult tasks with a computer which they may never have used before, and at the same time tell you all about what they are thinking! There may be two of you, and one of them. You know all about computers and they stand a fair chance of making a fool of themselves. This is an intimidating situation for them and you must do your best to put them at their ease by not seeming too knowledgeable, by not presenting yourself as an 'expert' and so on.

Silences

If the user stops talking and you are stuck for questions the best bet is simply to ask the user 'What are you doing now?'

The involved designer

Cooperative Evaluation is designed for use by designers. Having designers evaluate their own system means that they directly experience the users' problems. This provides a depth of understanding that is difficult to achieve when the evaluation is carried out by some third party. It also removes the time-consuming necessity to explain the system to a third party evaluator and for them to report back.

In our experience designers are always surprised by the problems users have. However, it is remarkably rare for designers to become defensive about their work in this situation. This is because the users are not asked to pass evaluative judgements on the system. Rather, they are trying to perform tasks set by the designer and in doing so provide valuable insights about recognisable design issues. Of course, every effort must be made to remain detached in the face of direct or implied criticism. If you find this difficult you should get someone else to actually run the session and take a passive role as observer.

See Chapter 3 for further trouble-shooting hints.

2.5.5   Debriefing

When the user has finished the set tasks you should take some time to talk to them about the session. Keep recording during this time; some of the most interesting comments come out at this stage. You should have some questions prepared. Some will be very open ended, e.g. 'What was the best/worst thing about the prototype', 'What most needs changing'. Some should be more specific e.g. 'Should the default value for ... be ... or ...'. You might also like to ask them to comment on the Cooperative Evaluation session itself: did they find the recording equipment intrusive, did you use the right tasks, was the prototype realistic enough? If you are testing with a number of users it may be useful to prepare a questionnaire and to get them to write the answers to these questions. Chapter 3 includes an example of such a questionnaire as Figure 3.3.

It will often not be possible to arrange two meetings with your users. If it is, it can be very valuable to talk to them after you have analysed your results and decided what improvements are to be made. One alternative is to arrange a meeting at which all the users involved in testing a particular prototype get together with the design team to review the problems observed and possible solutions. As well as serving as a check on your interpretation of what happened, this can have valuable 'managerial' advantages as a further opportunity for users and designers to get together and understand each other's point of view. Chapter 3 documents how this was done at Information Dimensions Inc. as a 'round table discussion'.

2.6   Summarise your observations

Given the time constraints generally in operation in an industrial setting we do not recommend that you spend a great deal of time listening in detail to the recordings of the sessions with users. You will certainly not have time to produce a written transcript. The main function of these tapes is to act as a back-up for you if there are details of the session that you can't remember but feel are very important to get exactly right. They can also be used to provide very concrete demonstrations of user problems during presentations to other designers or to senior management. Such demonstrations often prove to be more convincing sources of support for change than formal statistics about usability.

Primarily then, you will be working from your notes and your memory of the test session. Bearing this in mind, it is important to find time after each user testing session to pull your thoughts together and check your notes so that nothing important is forgotten.

The interaction session will provide you two basic kinds of information about the user's experience of usability. We refer to these two broad kinds of data as *unexpected behaviour* and *user comments*.

Unexpected behaviour is where the users do something the designer did not intend them to do. For example, the user might type in an inappropriate sequence of commands or data, they may use commands in an unexpectedly creative way, or they may use several commands when a shorter sequence would have done. These kinds of data are very important because they highlight a mismatch between how the designer expected the system to be used and how the user actually uses it. If you yourself are the designer then these should be relatively obvious to you during the session.

Comments are subjective comments or evaluations of the interface. These can be both positive and negative ('It's nice the way you can do that without having to type the whole thing again', 'That seemed to take a lot of effort', 'I don't like having to do that twice' and so on). These are very important sources of data too because they reflect the users' experiences with the system. Although they may be performing perfectly well with the system and behaving just as you expect, nevertheless, they may be experiencing the interaction as awkward, clumsy or effortful.

One useful way to proceed is to use your notes to make a list of the incidents in the form of an inventory containing a summary description of the comments and unexpected behaviour which occurred. This can include references to where in the tape they can be found. Having gathered these data together, attempt to find common themes that relate them.

A word of caution is in order here. A natural way of thinking about the problems a user had is in terms of redesign. As you see the user having problems you will think of possible solutions to those problems. This is the great strength of Cooperative Evaluation. The danger is to think that the first solution that comes to mind is the only solution. This is particularly true of solutions suggested by the user which are much better thought of as part of the *symptoms* of the problem. Thinking about possible solutions to problems as they arise is natural and important as a way of clarifying your ideas about what the problem is, but you should avoid prematurely committing yourself to a particular change to the design. Redesign should only proceed when you have the 'big picture' of all the problems with the prototype. Also if you are working as part of a design team it should be a collaborative effort involving all members of the team.

Another question is which of the problems identified should be fixed. Very often there will be one or two serious problems that can be identified immediately. If so, the required changes should be made and the new version re-evaluated. Some judgement will need to be made about the seriousness of a problem and whether the cost of fixing it is justifiable.

Finally, how should redesign proceed? Design is a skilled and creative process and you will have your own methods. One technique that we have found useful, however, is outlined below. This involves viewing the problem from two complementary perspectives, the *system perspective* and the *user perspective*. The technique is illustrated by means of an example below.

The <ESC> key problem

Users of a bibliographic database tool are provided with an area at the bottom of the screen where they can display references and page through them by pressing the <RET> key. Each press of the key advances the user on to the next reference. If the user browses to the very last reference then he/she will be taken back to the command menu automatically. If at any time before this the user wishes to abandon his/her browsing and go back to the command menu, he/she can press the <ESC> key. A common problem observed in this situation is that users get returned to the main menu automatically but nevertheless press the <ESC> key. This has the effect of exiting them from the command menu, closing the current selection and closing the current database.

(i) The system-centred perspective

This problem could potentially be interpreted as caused by failures at several different levels of system design.

- It could be interpreted as a problem with the use of the <ESC> key. If <ESC> was used to exit the main menu then perhaps it should not have also been used to exit the display browser.
- It could be interpreted as a failure to provide the user with sufficient feedback about which is the active window and when they have reached the end of the current display.
- It could be interpreted as the provision of non-intuitive functionality. Perhaps the user should not be returned to the main menu automatically.

Each of these interpretations represents a valid causal analysis from a system perspective and each suggests a design solution. For example, clearer marking of the active window, or perhaps a beep when the last item is displayed, maybe a different command key could be used and so on. The issue is not which interpretation is correct but rather what level of intervention would best meet the user's needs.

(ii) The user-centred perspective

When considering this perspective it is useful to ask yourself why the user behaved in the way he/she did? A superficial answer is to say that the user accidentally pressed <ESC>. But this is little more than a restatement of the problem. If we take the analysis a little further and ask 'Why did the user accidentally press <ESC>?' the reason we come up with is that the user did not notice the return to the main menu. If we pursue the question a little further and ask 'Why didn't the user notice the return to the main menu?' the answer that suggests itself is that the user did not notice returning to the main menu because he/she was not *expecting* to be returned to it. Normally in this situation the user has to press <ESC> in order to achieve this; only on the comparatively few occasions that they happen to be looking at the last reference are they automatically returned. In addition since the user's task at this point is browsing the selected references, their attention will be on the displayed reference and not on the main menu. One solution might be to make it a requirement for the user always to press <ESC> if they want to return to the main menu. This is not a satisfactory solution from a user perspective, however, because pressing <ESC> when the last reference is being viewed would be perceived by the user as unnecessary; after all, there is nothing else the user can do in this situation except return to the main menu. The user might reasonably expect the system to anticipate this *redundant* command. A creative line of reasoning from the user perspective at this point is to consider how the <ESC> command could be made *necessary* on the 'last' reference. The answer is to abandon the idea of a 'last' reference. If the user is provided with a *wrap-around* browse which redisplays the 'first' reference once the 'last' reference has been displayed, then the concept of a last reference is redundant and in that context it makes perfect sense to the user to have to explicitly press <ESC> to return to the main menu and because the user controls when to return to the main menu, then such a return cannot go unnoticed. This solution is creative and powerful because not only does it fix the design problem but it fixes it in a way which provides new functionality to the user. It will, however, place an extra demand on the user, namely, recognising when they have viewed all of the selections. This can be ameliorated by numbering the selection items.

2.7   Concluding comments

This chapter has described how to perform a Cooperative Evaluation session: how to recruit representative users, how to select appropriate tasks, how to run the session and how to summarise your observations. Appendix 1 is designed to be photocopied and used to actually run the session. We strongly recommend that you do this.

One thing that everyone who has used this kind of method agrees on is that designers are *always* surprised at the way users behave. There is no point in embarking on this exercise if you are not willing to change your design on the basis of what you find. If on the other hand you are open to the ideas that will arise from Cooperative Evaluation you will gain a new understanding of the way users think that will be of value now and beyond the current design project.

3 A case study: how Cooperative Evaluation was introduced at Information Dimensions Inc.

by Jeanne Haber, research by Lora Davenport and Jeanne Haber

3.1 Topics covered in this chapter

- Introduction to *BASISPLUS*
- Training designers
- Where we started
- Preparing a Cooperative Evaluation session
- Finding people to take part in the sessions
- Doing on-line Cooperative Evaluation
- At the end of the session
- Evaluating the results
- Using the data
- Tips on gaining the support of management
- A new role for human factors personnel

In 1989 Peter Wright and Andrew Monk began distributing copies of instructions for doing Cooperative Evaluation. These instructions were known as 'The York Manual'. Lora Davenport attended a talk by Peter Wright about Cooperative Evaluation at the CHI'89 conference in Texas. She obtained a copy of the manual and, with Jeanne Haber, proceeded to develop its use at Information Dimensions Inc. Their research went considerably further than the original manual and has now evolved as a whole new philosophy for the management of human factors work. This chapter is a case study tracing the development of this research. It serves to illustrate how Cooperative Evaluation can be customised to fit the needs of a particular company. Obviously every company has different aims and constraints, however, their experiences are clearly generalisable. In addition, many of their ideas have been incorporated in Chapter 2 and Appendix 1.

3.2 Introduction

BASISPLUS is a relational document retrieval system that handles both conventional records and continuous or sectioned textual documents up to thousands of pages long. This case study shows how we tested one of its interfaces called USE/SCREEN.

USE/SCREEN was originally designed to search, update, add and delete conventional and relatively short textual documents. It needed the added capability of handling very long, sectioned documents (such as on-line books) and to be moved into a Graphical User Interface (GUI) environment.

Before we made any changes to USE/SCREEN, we wanted to run it through usability testing and at the same time collect input on how our users would like it to change. Our goal was make it full-powered without destroying its popularity or ease of use.

We have used Cooperative Evaluation to conduct over 100 usability tests on several different *BASISPLUS* interfaces. Our case study summarises what we learned by using the Cooperative Evaluation method. It is derived from many Cooperative Evaluation sessions; however, for continuity, we will only show the USE/SCREEN interface in our illustration.

Before we begin the case study, we would like to talk about how we trained twelve interface designers to use the Cooperative Evaluation method and what we learned in the process.

3.3   Training designers

We began our training program by distributing excerpts from the York Manual (an earlier version of Chapter 2) via in-house electronic mail. We asked designers to read the manual as a class prerequisite. A few days later, we held a class in one of our company training rooms. These rooms are equipped with terminals that monitor what is happening on the instructor's terminal.

We chose one inexperienced designer to try to conduct a session, as all the others watched on-line. The instructor played 'everyuser' (a user given to frequent mood swings).

Designers were asked to make suggestions and ask questions during the training session. Then we gave them sample tasks and excerpts from the York Manual to study. A few days later we began practice sessions. The practice sessions gave designers a feel for the process and helped to identify problems in the tests themselves. During the practice sessions they divided into groups of three:

- A designer of the interface (to run the session)
- A designer to play the role of user
- A designer to observe

The observers stopped the practice sessions to point out mistakes or to make suggestions that would improve the dialogue. We attempted to rotate roles and tasks so that most of the designers had a chance to act as user, designer and observer at least once.

Designers running the sessions were assigned to interfaces they knew best.

However, the designers acting as users tested products they had not worked on. This brought about some interesting side benefits.

All three designers became more sensitive to the user's perspective.

- The one acting as user, because they actually felt the confusion.
- The two others because they respected their fellow designer; i.e. this program is written for users much less skilled than John. John is having problems. The problems must be in the design.

A few of these mixed-project practice sessions turned into spontaneous, highly focused brain-storming sessions.

3.4   Where we started

Figure 3.1 illustrates the interface we tested and summarises why we chose to test it. As we mentioned earlier, USE/SCREEN is a very popular interface, especially for novice or occasional users, but it was designed to handle conventional records with fields no longer than 16,000 characters. We wanted to adapt it to handle huge books with multiple chapters and sections.

3.5   Preparing a Cooperative Evaluation session

For our first usability tests we copied tutorials out of our documentation and simply asked the user to follow the tutorials. However, most of our users skip the tutorials and try to learn on their own, so we wanted to create less structured tasks for the user to do. After several different attempts, this is the process we think produces the best set of tasks for the user to work through:

- Outline objectives
- Discover specific areas where user input would be helpful
- Outline test scope
- Storyboard session to make it gradually more task-oriented
- Plan optional tasks for advanced users

3.5.1   Step 1: Outline objectives

For each interface we tested we had specific issues we wanted users to comment on. This was our list for USE/SCREEN.

- Get users' first reaction to the screen and the action line.
- Show them explicitly how to do a Match.
- Find out if the default Show action ($>$) is what they expect (want) to happen?
- Find out how they want to scroll the text stream.
- See if they can remember how to do a Match after an interruption.
- Does learning how to do one action teach how to do the others?

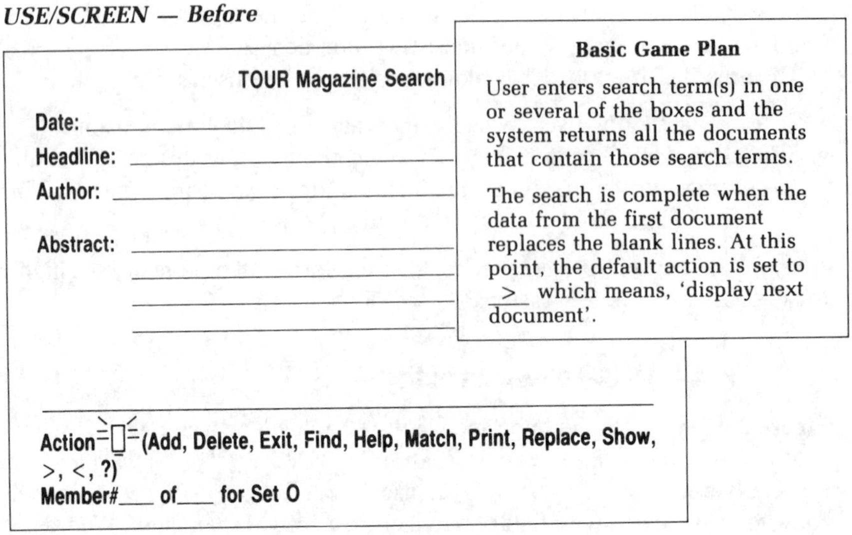

Figure 3.1
The problem,
modifying the
USE/SCREEN
interface for large
documents

USE/SCREEN — Before

TOUR Magazine Search

Date: _____

Headline: _____

Author: _____

Abstract: _____
_____
_____
_____

_____
Action=☐(Add, Delete, Exit, Find, Help, Match, Print, Replace, Show,
>, <, ?)
Member#___ of___ for Set 0

Basic Game Plan

User enters search term(s) in one
or several of the boxes and the
system returns all the documents
that contain those search terms.

The search is complete when the
data from the first document
replaces the blank lines. At this
point, the default action is set to
> which means, 'display next
document'.

Before the advent of long textual documents . . .

The default action after a Match was > (show next document).

There was no difference between scrolling text or any other
kind of data. (No sections or chapters to worry about and
probably a limited amount of scrolling going on anyway.) All
scrolling could reasonably be managed by function keys.

Once the first document was displayed it was most likely a user
would want to move through the set one document at a time
or perhaps choose an action such as Replace or Delete.
Therefore, we left the cursor on the action bar rather than
placing it up in the document. Also, there was no way to
predict what box a user would want to scroll, so it was logical
to wait for the user to show you.

But the defaults were not suited to textual applications . . .

In a textual application, it is very likely a user would want to
scroll the text before moving on to the next document, but to
do so with the current defaults meant he had to arrow up to
the text box before he could begin scrolling. This seemed like
unnecessary work to people accustomed to textual
applications.

Also, there were suddenly many new ways to scroll: by next
or previous occurrence of the search term, chapter, window,
line, page, etc. In addition, users like the ability to jump to
the first or last line, occurrence, chapter etc. It is difficult to
remember function keys for all these variations, so we needed
another alternative.

- Test secondary action lines. Do new users notice the format change? Are the instructions confusing?

3.5.2   Step 2: Discover specific areas where user input would be helpful

Go over the objectives and get specific. Discuss known usability issues and list fixes already in progress. Discover open and closed issues. For example, in USE/SCREEN we did not want to change the basic 'fill in the blank' format because we knew it was popular and easy to learn. But we were willing to change action names, default cursor location, messages, on-line help and scrolling methods. Some of our specific USE/SCREEN questions were:

- How would users prefer to scroll? With keys only, or with commands and keys? Where should the cursor be placed by default? Should the default action continue to be 'Next Document' or should we change it?
- What would be the most intuitive way to introduce the concept of chapters and sections within the text stream? Where would they look for the Table of Contents? What kind of status information would they need? Current document number? Total number of documents? Current chapter number? Total number of chapters?
- What kind of help would they need and how would they prefer to access it? Would they like to write their own help messages if the means were provided?

3.5.3   Step 3: Outline test scope

We began by outlining the test scope, which is a list of tasks we will ask the user to do, the 'task sheet'. This is not the same as the test objectives, which outlines what we want to *learn* during the tests. We found the users liked going over the task sheet before starting the first task but we were careful not to say too much and 'contaminate' our data by listing objectives as well (see Figure 3.2).

3.5.4   Step 4: Storyboard session to make it gradually more task oriented

For the USE/SCREEN test, we also wrote a storyboard so that our instructions would gradually be more task-oriented. This was to get a feel for how much time it took to learn basic steps. All USE/SCREEN functions (Match, Add, Delete, Replace, etc.) work the same way in that you:

1. Enter the first letter of the action you want to start (the main actions are replaced by specific sub-actions).
2. Enter your data.

Figure 3.2
Task sheet for
USE/SCREEN

USE/SCREEN   Task sheet

Part 1.   Match and Show Documents

Select Match action.
Enter search term.
Move through set.
Scroll data.

Part 2.   Add a New Document

Match an existing document.
Select Add action.
Enter new data.
Execute the Add.

Part 3.   Edit a Document in a Result Set

Create a result set.
Move to the document you want to change.
Select Replace action.
Change and replace the document.

Part 4.   Delete a Document

Move to the document you want to delete.
Select Delete action.
Verify and execute delete.

We started the USE/SCREEN test with explicit directions to do a Match (a simple search). When the documents were found, we deliberately diverted the user's attention to scrolling and status bar issues. After working with scrolling for a while, they turned the page and saw the instruction 'Do another Match'. A little more than half of them remembered what to do. The others tried to enter their search terms before they returned to the action bar and entered an M. Later we told them to 'Start an Add'. All of them correctly guessed they needed to return to the action line and enter an A. Finally, we asked them to 'Create a result set'. This meant they would have to remember the word 'Match' as well as to begin by entering the letter M.

3.5.5   *Step 5: Write optional tasks for advanced users*

Prepare for the experienced user by having some additional questions or exercises ready (see the section 'Doing on-line Cooperative Evaluation').

3.6   Finding people to take part in the sessions

Before we took our tests to the user community, we tried them out in-house to make sure they were written clearly and to find out how long they would take to run. We asked people from other departments to take part in these sessions. This gave the developers more practice and gave us valuable input on the procedure itself.

From the outset, we never had any difficulty getting people to participate. Our company cohosts biannual user group meetings in different cities around the United States and in our home office in Columbus, Ohio. When the meetings are out of town, we set up video cameras in hotel rooms. In Spring of 1990, the meeting was in Columbus so we were able to hold the test sessions in our own Research and Development offices.

3.7 Doing on-line Cooperative Evaluation

We found the introductory comments suggested in the manual were very effective. They put users at ease and explained the objectives concisely. We also appreciated the section on different kinds of users to expect. These are a few we discovered on our own:

Tunnel-vision user	Some of our users preferred doing everything by command and were not open-minded about finding the best way to do the same tasks in a screen or GUI environment. It seemed they would object to anything new. We addressed this problem by providing more details about the kind of programs we would be testing and by trying to match users to environments they were accustomed to.
People-pleaser	We had to discount the data from one session because the user seemed to be trying to say what he thought we wanted to hear. He assumed any confusion was his fault.
User who fakes understanding	A few of our users were embarrassed to admit they did not understand what to do next. When we reviewed the tapes, it was difficult to tell at what point we lost them.
Expert (aka dangerous) user	Many of our users were very comfortable using new software and had their own agenda. One man left the program and began moving around in the system software. We learned to set limits. Users who could show us new ways they would use the software were very helpful, but not users who wanted to experiment with the equipment on our time. In order to set reasonable boundaries, we prepared some more advanced tasks to suggest if necessary.

Overall, we did not have trouble getting people to 'think aloud'. We found the open-ended questions suggested in the York Manual worked very well. We used phrases such as: 'What did you expect to happen?' 'Why do you think that's confusing?' 'What would you rather the message said?' 'How would you design it?'

3.8   At the end of the session

The following are some of the ways we collected data after the on-line tests. We conducted debriefing dialogues and added:

- Written or on-line post-test surveys
- Round-table discussions involving all test participants

3.8.1   The value of debriefing

We found that debriefing gave us time to go back and clear up misunderstandings. Being on a strict time schedule, it was also handy to be able to say, 'We can talk about that later'. It is useful to take a few minutes before debriefing to look over your hurried notes and learn where you need clarification.

3.8.2   The value of a post-test survey

These written questionnaires give us a way to poll users on specific questions and to provide immediate feedback at the round table. Our post-test surveys address:

- General preferences
- Specific design issues
- How the user feels about the system
- Which suggestions he feels strongly enough about to rate as:
  'What I liked most'
  'What I would most like to change'

Figure 3.3 illustrates the questions asked in the USE/SCREEN example.

3.8.3   Round-table discussions

Because we have a large and diverse user population, we added a round-table session to bring all test participants together at the end of the week. We wanted users to hear how others reacted to the same test and to debate their differences of opinion on tape. We invited upper management to attend so that they could hear users' reactions to the test process itself. These are some of the benefits of the round table.

- Users became aware that we work for many masters and that there are different visions of 'easy-to-use'.
- Users were able to support their points-of-view with details and examples we did not hear the first time around. They also liked having some time to think about the experience and to sum up their impressions in their own words.
- We were able to get a read on some group priorities.

Figure 3.3
Sample post-test
questionnaire

USE/SCREEN
Sample Post-Test Survey

Test Date:
Designer:
Name(s):
Company:

Multiple Choice

1. Which category is closest to your job description?
   a. End User b. Data Base Analyst c. Software Analyst

2. Which environment best describes the interface you work with daily?
   a. Screen/action bar   b. Menu driven
   c. Point and Click (GUI)   d. Command

3. In general, do you like the USE/SCREEN Interface?
   a. Yes   b. No

4. Should the cursor move to the first field (or a default field) when you enter an M, A or R?
   a. Yes   b. No

5. Would you like to define a default Tab sequence to determine the cursor path?
   a. Yes   b. No

6. During Show, when you press [ENTER] to get to the next document, should the cursor remain where it was?
   a. Yes   b. No

7. During Show, when you change the member number and the action is >, should the system put up:
   a. the member you specified?
   b. the member you specified + 1?

8. During Show, when you reach the last document, should the > automatically change to <?
   a. Yes   b. No

9. Should you be able to scroll text by entering letters in the action box, or is function key scrolling sufficient?
   a. Keys only   b. Keys or commands

10. Were you confused about when to use arrows and when to use the Tab key?
    a. Yes   b. No

11. Should there be DBA written PF2 help (sample term, legal lists, etc.) for each field?
    a. Yes   b. No

12. Should you be able to Tab through to the next page, without using the Next Page key?
    a. Yes   b. No

13. Were the Add and Replace prompts confusing?
    a. Yes   b. No

14. Was the Delete prompt confusing?
    a. Yes   b. No

15. If the cursor is in the action box, should the [RET] key act exactly like [ENTER]?
    a. Yes   b. No

Essay Questions

What did you like most about USE/SCREEN?

What, if anything, would you like to change?

Other comments or suggestions on USE/SCREEN or on the Usability Test process:

Thank you for your participation!

- We heard, and more importantly management heard, many positive comments on the value of test process itself (see the section 'Tips on gaining the support of management').

3.9   Evaluating the results

We tried several different approaches to reviewing the video tapes and think the most productive is to watch them in small teams with worksheets and doughnuts. Watching tapes in groups of three or four makes it easier to decipher inaudible comments. Also you can:

- Identify and discuss different interpretations of the users' behaviour or source of confusion
- Quasi-agree on a list of problems that need to be addressed
- Brainstorm on ideas or solutions that come up spontaneously
- Learn from each other's mistakes and successes

3.9.1   *Management reports*

At IDI we have a single usability test analyst who also watches the tapes, reads all the designers' reports, and summarises the data for management. Summaries are comprised of a list of problems encountered most often and a compilation of user comments and suggestions on the post-test survey. This is how we introduced the content of the reports:

Cooperative Evaluation usability testing is not a study of numbers. Every user comment and question is valuable data, whether it is made by one person or 20. Comments that support program design are as important as those that point out problems; therefore, the only true test 'results' are the tapes themselves, which are played uncut in team meetings.

The purpose of compiling tape *summaries* is to look for trends and to provide test participants with a sample of the input we received.

Usability data divides into three broad categories: problems, suggestions and support.

It was relatively easy to compile a summary list of problems. We simply gave more weight to problems that occurred more than once or that caused the user a great deal of difficulty. Suggestions were harder to summarise. A good suggestion is a good suggestion, regardless of how many people it occurs to. To stay objective, we decided to include only those suggestions received in answer to the post-test survey question, 'What, if anything, would you like to change?' or that came up during the round-table discussion.

Some of the suggestions that arose when testing the USE/SCREEN interface are summarised in Figure 3.4.

Suggestions for redesign of USE/SCREEN

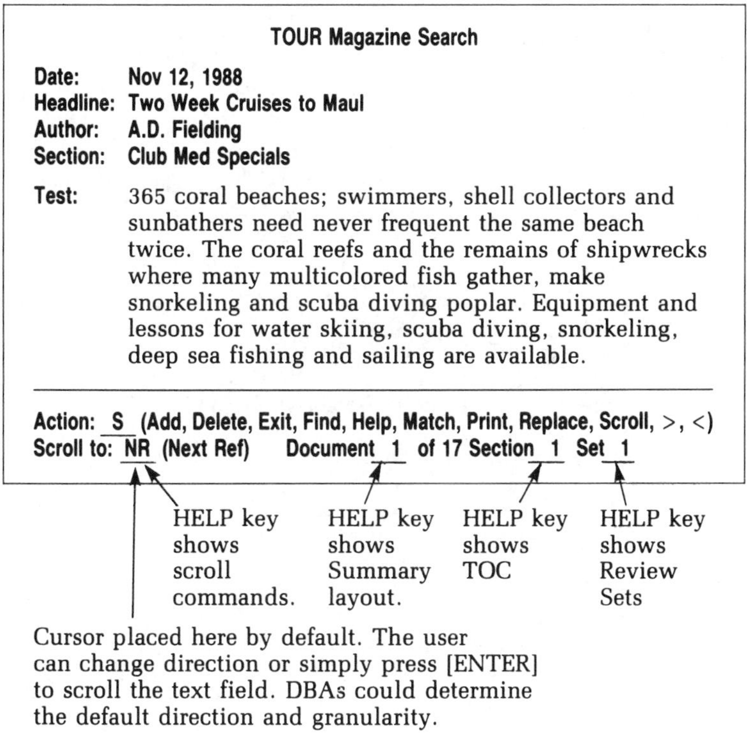

Figure 3.4
Suggestion for improving the USE/SCREEN interface

TOUR Magazine Search

Date: Nov 12, 1988
Headline: Two Week Cruises to Maul
Author: A.D. Fielding
Section: Club Med Specials

Test: 365 coral beaches; swimmers, shell collectors and sunbathers need never frequent the same beach twice. The coral reefs and the remains of shipwrecks where many multicolored fish gather, make snorkeling and scuba diving poplar. Equipment and lessons for water skiing, scuba diving, snorkeling, deep sea fishing and sailing are available.

Action: S (Add, Delete, Exit, Find, Help, Match, Print, Replace, Scroll, >, <)
Scroll to: NR (Next Ref)   Document 1 of 17 Section 1 Set 1

HELP key   HELP key   HELP key   HELP key
shows   shows   shows   shows
scroll   Summary   TOC   Review
commands.   layout.   Sets

Cursor placed here by default. The user can change direction or simply press [ENTER] to scroll the text field. DBAs could determine the default direction and granularity.

3.10   Using the data

This section offers tips on turning suggestions and complaints into action items by making drawings, categorising data and preparing cooperative design sessions.

3.10.1   Drawings

Drawings are a good way of summarising conclusions drawn from the data as possible recommendations for redesign. Using free-hand drawing emphasises that these are suggestions and not the final design. Figure 3.4 was created from such a drawing.

3.10.2   Categorisation

The video tapes returned many different kinds of data. We found it was useful to turn comments into actions by grouping issues into the following categories:

- Cursor movement issues
- Terminology issues
- Structural issues (Too many layers? Not enough?)
- Work-flow issues (Designed to support user's task?)

3.10.3   Cooperative design sessions

The success of the round-table sessions led us to develop what we call Cooperative Design sessions. These are group sessions where we show paper drawings of possible solutions and again invite users and employees in other parts of the company to openly debate their strengths and weaknesses. Figure 3.5 is a sample agenda for a Cooperative Design session.

Figure 3.5
Agenda for a
Cooperative Design
session

USE/SCREEN Design Evaluation

I.   **Objectives and Procedure**
   - What we hope to accomplish
   - How we run Cooperative Design sessions

II. **Presentation of Designs**
   - How it is now
   - Changes to status line
   - Changes to help
   - 3 possible designs

III. **Discussion**
   - Pros and cons of each design
   - Design changes suggested by users at IDEA
   - Other usability issues raised at IDEA

3.11   Tips on gaining the support of management

Before new techniques or methods are introduced into a company management have to be convinced that the investment in personnel and other resources will result in tangible benefits. Cooperative Evaluation is a low cost option, so it was relatively easy to convince management to agree to a small scale trial. Everything that we did was documented so we were able to provide hard facts about the real costs and benefits in this trial. When it came to introducing Cooperative Evaluation as a standard procedure, a strong case could then be made. It is particularly important to provide management with documentation on the side-benefits of doing Cooperative Evaluation usability testing. Some of these benefits are listed below.

- Customers like it. Just meeting the sharp personable articulate men and women working on their code instils confidence.
- Cameras, notes, questions, surveys all do much more to convey genuine interest in the customers' point of view than any presentation or 'town-hall' format attempted in the past.
- Designers like meeting the customers. The tapes show that the designers are enjoying themselves and are very capable of discussing issues directly. They like speaking with the customers one-to-one.
- Designers have a much better understanding of the user's perspective which can carry over into future designs.
- The tests themselves have other uses that justify the time it takes to write them. They:
  — Improve in-house communications and training
  — Help us develop better tutorials and marketing demonstrations
  — Result in better design notes
  — Document the design evolution

Inviting management to round-table discussions is also a very powerful way of communicating the value of a technique like Cooperative Evaluation.

3.12   Conclusion — a new role for human factors personnel

In conclusion, the benefits of Cooperative Evaluation usability testing have been many, and the investment and risk minimal. In a very short time the procedure has moved from 'good ideas' to standard operating procedure at IDI. It is worth noting that using Cooperative Evaluation has subtly changed the role of human factors personnel at IDI. Before the introduction of Cooperative Evaluation human factors personnel had a more direct evaluative role. Too often we were brought in late on in a design project when it was difficult to make any changes. Getting in early on in the design process meant being a part of the design team and there simply were not sufficient resources

Figure 3.6
(a) The old model of human factors support, human factors people act as a buffer between user and designers; (b) when users are brought together using a technique such as Cooperative Evaluation, human factors people have a new role as facilitators

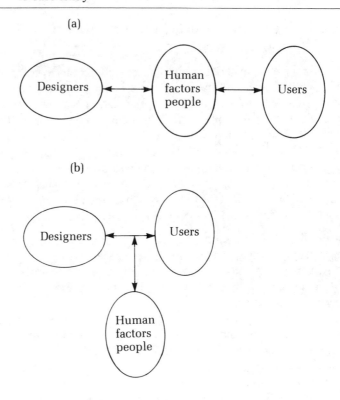

to do this with every project. Cooperative Evaluation allows the human factors personnel to take a new role as the people that enable and facilitate usability testing. This is illustrated in Figure 3.6.

Instead of human factors people acting as a buffer between designers their role becomes one of enabling designers and users to get together. This involves training designers to use Cooperative Evaluation, helping with the recruitment of users and advising on, or carrying out, the management of the whole process.

4 Validating the technique

4.1 Topics covered in this chapter

- Introduction to the experiments
- Study 1 — the evaluation of an interface with known problems
- Study 2 — the evaluation of your own design
- Summary and conclusions

In Chapter 3 you have already seen how the technique has been successfully introduced into a company. This chapter will report on some laboratory experiments which show

(a) the technique can be used effectively by people who are not human factors specialists and

(b) the technique can be used by designers to discover unexpected problems in their own designs.

4.2 Introduction

We have made two important claims about the advantage to practitioners of Cooperative Evaluation over and above other techniques.

- Software engineers with little or no human factors experience can learn to use this technique very easily.
- Designers, with the aid of this technique, can evaluate their own prototypes effectively.

The value to software developers of such a technique is clear. Firstly, by reducing the reliance on human factors specialists, Cooperative Evaluation can take place quickly and cheaply, solving the problem of the evaluation bottleneck often experienced by companies. Secondly, by involving the designer in Cooperative Evaluation we bring the user and the designer closer together. This has the twofold value of increasing the designer's awareness of the target user population while at the same time enhancing the profile of the company's quality assurance techniques. This in turn makes the customer more committed to the product.

In this chapter we report some validation work that we have carried out to substantiate these claims. The work takes the form of two empirical studies carried out at the University of York. The aim was to provide some quantitative support for our claims. In the final analysis, however, we recognise that the real proof comes from using Cooperative Evaluation in an industrial setting. In Chapter 3 we reported on one company's experience of using Cooperative Evaluation in an industrial setting. We would argue that the laboratory work to be reported in this chapter taken together with the industrial experience reported in Chapter 3, provide good evidence that Cooperative Evaluation is not only a cost-effective but also a practical technique for iterative, user-centred evaluation. Readers who wish to have more detail about the studies reported in this chapter are referred to a recent paper in the *International Journal of Man—Machine Studies* by Wright and Monk entitled 'A cost-effective evaluation method for use by designers' (Wright and Monk, 1991a).

Study 1 examines the claim that Cooperative Evaluation can be used effectively and after only minimal training, by people without human factors skills. Study 2 examines the claim that the technique can be used by designers to evaluate their own interfaces.

Both studies employ post-graduate students as experimental subjects. These students were enrolled on an MSc course in Information Processing run by the Department of Computer Science at York University. The academic backgrounds of the students are varied; some have undergraduate degrees in arts and humanities, some in sciences. The aim of the MSc course is to provide them with a basic conversion training in computer science. Many students who finish this course will go on to work as software engineers in industry. Thus, while our subjects were not highly trained software engineers, they were reasonably representative of our target population in terms of their general aptitude and their academic background. The two studies to be reported were carried out with two different intakes to the course separated by one year. Thus no one subject took part in both studies.

4.3   Study 1

Synopsis

Q. Can Cooperative Evaluation be used effectively by non-human factors specialists?

A. Yes it can. The non-specialists do not do as well as specialists, but with the absolute minimum of self-training and minimum use of resources they can still identify enough usability problems to make the exercise cost-effective.

4.3.1   *Introduction to Study 1*

In designing this study we were aware of the difficulties faced by designers in industry. Usually they have a very limited budget in terms of time and resources dedicated to human factors evaluation. We were aware that most designers would not have the time available to spend many hours learning how to carry out Cooperative Evaluation. We were also aware that they would probably have difficulty recruiting users for the evaluation. With these constraints in mind we were interested to see how well our students could do when given only minimal self-instruction on the Cooperative Evaluation technique and when they had access to only one user.

As instruction in the use of Cooperative Evaluation, our students were given an early version of the Cooperative Evaluation manual presented in Chapter 2 of this book. They were given the manual one week before they were scheduled to carry out the evaluation and asked to read it as part of their normal course work. For the evaluation itself they were provided with one novice user for a period of one hour. We felt that this represented a minimal user testing situation that should be possible even in the most austere of industrial settings.

Twenty-seven students took part in this study, forming thirteen teams (twelve teams of 2 and one team of 3).

The system the students were asked to evaluate was an in-house bibliographic database called REF. The reason for choosing an existing system rather than asking the students to design something themselves was as follows. The REF system was a product which had undergone many user testing studies as part of our on-going research into human−computer interaction at York. It had been used in a previous study which had collected over 100 hours of data from several users who used the system as part of their everyday work. It had also been used by the present authors in their own development of the Cooperative Evaluation technique. In fact, the transcripts included as training material in Appendix 2 of this book are transcripts of studies evaluating the REF system.

Because of the large amount of work that had been done with REF, we felt that as human factors specialists, we knew practically all of the usability problems associated with REF. These had been collected together in an inventory of usability problems which formed a corpus of data against which we could judge the effectiveness of our students in this experiment. By using the REF system for this study we would thus be able not only to compare the reports generated by our students with each other, but also with the larger corpus collected by human factors specialists. In this way we could provide a quantitative measure of how effective the Cooperative Evaluation technique was in the hands of our students.

There are two disadvantages to using an existing system for our study. The first is that since the evaluators of the system are not the designers, then our claim that Cooperative Evaluation can be used by designers to test their own products is not tested in this study. That is why this claim is tested separately in the second study reported later in the chapter. The second objection is that because the students have to familiarise themselves with the system and the user's tasks, it is possible that some of the problems they identify stem from this experience rather than the experience of talking with users. This would be a serious objection if we were making strong claims about the fact that the problems identified by the students were in some sense characteristic of the users they were testing. But for our purposes here, all we are interested in is the number of problems that can be identified by the students as a product of the Cooperative Evaluation process in total. After all, we are interested in identifying as many usability problems as possible whether they are experienced by the user or the evaluator. Even in a situation where a designer tested their own design, we would expect them to identify several problems merely from walking the system through the tasks intended for the user. This in itself is a valuable exercise which helps the designer focus in on potential areas of difficulty for the user.

REF is a menu-based bibliographic database. The records in the database had several fields that could be searched and modified. These included the authors' names, the date of publication, the title of the book or journal article, the publisher, keyword and classification information, and also where the source book or article could be found (i.e. whether it was in the department library and so on). The system keeps a time-stamped log of the user's key depressions and the state of the display windows.

The top level menu includes options for making a selection from a library, inserting a new reference into the library, altering a selected reference and so on. Users made menu selections by typing the first letter of their menu choice, whereupon the menu was partially overlaid by another menu or a data entry field. In addition to the menus and data entry fields, there was a window at the bottom of the screen for displaying selected references. There was also a smaller window in the top right hand corner of the screen for displaying

Figure 4.1
A typical REF screen

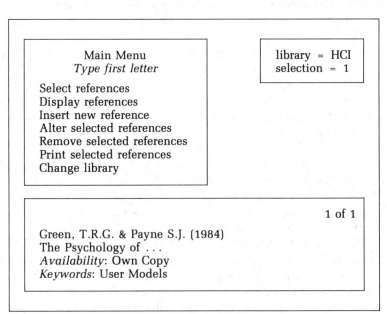

the name of the reference database currently being used (this is referred to as the current library) and the number of references currently selected from the library.

Figure 4.1 shows a schematic diagram of a typical REF screen after the user has been searching for a reference. At the bottom of the screen is the reference that the user had selected. It gives the title of a paper, the names of the authors, the year of publication and other information that has been entered by the user such as keyword.

At the top left of the screen is the main menu. By choosing the first letter of any item on this menu the user can carry out the operations specified, usually via some subsidiary menus. In the top right hand corner is a window which tells the user how many references they have currently selected and the name of the library they are currently working with.

For more information about the system the reader is referred to Appendix 2 which includes further illustrations of REF menus, descriptions of the dialogue structure and also transcripts of people cooperatively evaluating the system.

4.3.2   Details of the procedures

Synopsis

Q. How did we test these ideas?

A. The student software engineers were given some tasks to carry out with the REF system. Once they were familiar with the system they were taught how to do Cooperative Evaluation. They were then given one user to help them with a Cooperative Evaluation session. The students were asked to record the problems their user experienced. This list of problems was then compared with studies carried out by human factors specialists to decide how good the students had been at discovering the serious problems known to exist with REF.

The study was carried out in two sessions, separated by a week. Each session lasted 2 hours.

In the first session the students familiarised themselves with the REF system. They carried out a set of six tasks which involved selecting references, pruning down these selections and altering fields in individual references. The tasks used in this study are presented in Figure 4.2.

These same six tasks were also used by the students in the actual Cooperative Evaluation session. By familiarising themselves in this first session with how the tasks should be carried out, the students were able to identify their user's problems more easily. If, of course, the students had been the actual designers of the system this familiarisation stage would not have been necessary.

The students studied the Cooperative Evaluation manual in between the

Figure 4.2
The tasks given to
users in Study 1

1. Load the HCI library.

2. Find the title of the article by Kato.
   title = . . .

3. Find the title of the only paper by Thomas and Gould.
   title = . . .

4. Find the Kato paper again and add 'on-line help' to the keywords.

5. Alter Green and Payne (1984) by adding 'learnability' to the keywords and 'library copy' to the availability.

6. Find the year of publication of the most recent references to 'software design'.
   year of publication = . . .

first and second sessions. In the second session they were provided with a naive user for a maximum of one hour during which time they carried out a Cooperative Evaluation session. They used an audio cassette tape to record their conversations with the user. In addition they had access to the log of user input to the system. This log was produced by the system and comprised a trace of all user input and its effect on the system. The input recorded included

Figure 4.3
An example of a
system log

Session 1, 21.05.92, user = PCW

time	user input	active pane code	label	type
0:0.00		1	main menu	menu
0:30.50	S			
0:31.61		5	select by what?	menu
0:35.32	n			
0:35.92		6	selection by author	text
0:37.10	G			
0:37.32	o			
0:37.53	u			
0:37.71	l			
0:37.90	d			
0:38.24	<RET>			
0:38.35		66	selection = 12	status box
0:38.37		1	main menu	menu

menu choices and data entered. The output recorded what menus were active on the screen. Figure 4.3 shows an example of such a system log.

In the first row is some information entered by the evaluator. The first column records the elapsed time in minutes, seconds and fractions of a second. The second column records the user keystrokes. The third column records a code for which of the various menus and windows is active. The fourth column records the type of the active pane.

Each student wrote an independent report for the purpose of assessment. These were read individually and the problems each team reported were listed. This listing took the form of an inventory of scenarios describing situations in which the behaviour of the system caused the user problems. Each scenario comprised a one-line summary of the problem and a more detailed description of the user's input and the effect it has on the system. For example:

> **Scenario 19: print (immediate) understood as a display command**
> **Detailed description:** The user intends to display the current selection. The main menu is showing. The user types P for (P)rint. This generates a new menu asking for a decision about whether to print to a (F)ile or to print (I)mmediately to the printer. The user presses (I) for immediate printout. The system returns to the main menu. No references are displayed.

4.3.3   The results of Study 1

Synopsis

Q. How well did the students do?

A. They did very well considering they evaluated REF with the help of only one user and had only minimal training in the technique. The students detected twenty-nine problems in total which amounts to all but four of the known problems in REF. Furthermore they were best at discovering really serious problems and not so good at discovering trivial ones.

Overall performance of the students

The students reported a total of twenty-nine different problems. Not all teams identified all twenty-nine problems, however. An average team identified 9.6 of the twenty-nine problems, although the variance between teams was quite high (standard deviation = 3.04). For example, the best team detected fourteen problems while the two worst teams each detected five.

The variance between teams reflects in part the fact that many of the twenty-nine problems listed were very minor and idiosyncratic. For example, one of the problems was that a user attempted to make menu selections by using the cursor keys on the keyboard when in fact they needed to type in the initial letter of their menu choice. REF did not respond to this input and users did

Figure 4.4
Classification scheme
for the serious
problems and
frequency of
occurrence of various
problem types

problems involving complex task-action mapping	2
problems involving hard-to-reverse effects	3
problems involving unintended database changes	1
problems involving feedback about changes to libraries	2
problems involving feedback about outcome of search	2
total	10

not persist in trying to make choices in that way. In contrast some of the problems were more serious and more persistent, for example, some users accidentally abandoned searches or alterations resulting in a good deal of wasted time.

In order to focus our analysis on serious usability problems, problems that had no adverse consequences for the user (because the system simply did not respond) and problems that were easily resolved (such as whether or not the system accepted lowercase letters as menu choices) were removed from the problem list. Serious problems that were more difficult for the user to resolve or involved adverse or unnoticed effects on the database, were left on the list. These serious problems fell into five categories listed in Figure 4.4 along with the frequency of occurrence of each type.

The average hit rate for these ten problems was 45%. There were three serious problems that were detected by a large majority of teams (eight out of thirteen). Similarly there were four problems that most teams (eight out of thirteen) missed. This variance could reflect insensitivity in the technique, failure on the part of teams to report all problems or the fact that some problems, although serious, occur infrequently and may be related to individual differences between users. Some evidence for this latter view can be gained by considering the four problems that were detected by most teams compared with the four problems that were missed by most teams. This is done in Figures 4.5 and 4.6.

As can be seen from a consideration of Figure 4.6, for example, the user who failed to understand the ' < > year of publication' prompt (Scenario 31) may simply have been unfamiliar with these mathematical symbols. The problem of omitting the field name of a search parameter (Scenario 2c) also reflects individual differences between users. The team reporting this problem report that their user (unlike the users tested by other teams) was an experienced typist and often typed ahead of the system. If this interpretation of why Scenarios 2c and 31 are infrequently detected is correct, then the implication is that testing more than one user would reveal considerably more problems than testing one, particularly if users are deliberately chosen to be heterogeneous with respect to background, experience and skills.

The relatively small number of teams detecting Scenarios 7c and 16, is not

Scenario 12a: search by joint authors attempted

Detailed description: The user wishes to search for a reference with two authors. The user chooses to select by author name field and proceeds to type in the two authors' names joined by an '&'. The system in fact only supports searching by one author at a time. In order to achieve this effect the user must do two separate searches, one for each author. Nevertheless the system accepts the input and returns a zero current selection even though the target reference is present in the library. This can lead the user to wrongly conclude the reference is not available (see 6a below).

number of teams reporting the problem = 13 out of 13

Scenario 6a: unsuccessful search goes unnoticed

Detailed description: The user changes the size of the current selection by searching for a particular item. This can cause the current selection to be set to zero. The user fails to notice this and will carry out further actions (i.e. attempting to display the current selection) in the mistaken belief that some references are still selected.

number of teams reporting the problem = 12 out of 13

Scenario 9: feedback about menu choices goes unnoticed

Detailed description: The user wishes to alter the classification or availability of a reference. She selects the appropriate menus. These are multi-choice menus. The user selects an option. This is signalled to the user by the option being highlighted momentarily. She does not notice the highlighting and so selects the option again. Only when all the alterations are finally completed will the user find the option recorded several times on the newly altered reference. In order to rectify this the user must redo the alterations.

number of teams reporting the problem = 12 out of 13

Scenario 12b: no way of undoing a failed search

Detailed description: The user makes a sequence of searches on the same selection. Say, for example, searching by first author, then by second author and then by year of publication and then by keyword. Each successive search is intended to explore an increasingly smaller set of references. If one of the searches fails to find any references the selection is lost and the user cannot get back to that selection except by repeating the whole sequence over again.

number of teams reporting the problem = 8 out 13

Figure 4.5
The serious problems detected by eight or more groups in Study 1 (from Wright and Monk, 1991a, see Bibliography)

Figure 4.6
The serious problems
missed by eight or
more teams in Study
1 (from Wright and
Monk, 1991a, see
Bibliography)

Scenario 7c: alterations that are made are not saved

Detailed description: The user chooses the alter command from the main menu. This provides a subsidiary menu allowing her to choose DONE if no more alterations are to be made. She has several alterations to make and carries each of them out returning to the subsidiary menu each time. The alterations are shown on the displayed references. When she has no more alterations to make she presses <ESC> returning to the main menu without pressing DONE. This has the effect of aborting the alterations without saving them although they are still displayed as if they had been changed.

number of teams reporting the problem = 3 out of 13

Scenario 16: keyword changes are not displayed immediately

Detailed description: The user wishes to add a keyword to a reference. She selects the (A)lter option from the main menu and the (A)dd keyword option from the subsidiary menu. She types in the new keyword. She notices that the keywords of the reference displayed on the screen have not changed and presses <ESC> in order to attempt the alteration again.

number of teams reporting the problem = 3 out of 13

Scenario 2c: failure to type field name for search command

Detailed description: The user intends to search the library for a particular field and value (e.g. KEYWORD = design). The user chooses the search option and then goes directly to specifying the value of the field (i.e. design) without specifying the field itself (e.g. KEYWORD). The system takes the first letter of the input corresponding to a valid field as the intended field and the remainder as the value for that field. A search is conducted as normal. If no valid input is found nothing happens.

number of teams reporting the problem = 1 out of 13

Scenario 31: option for searching by < or > year goes unnoticed

Detailed description: The user wishes to search for all references in a library that were published before or after a certain date. She achieves this by repeated searches for successive years (e.g. YEAR OF PUBLICATION = 1983, YEAR OF PUBLICATION = 1984). She does not use the < > option that is provided.

number of teams reporting the problem = 1 out of 13

easily explicable in this way. Our tentative interpretation of this is that these are errors due to inconsistencies in the way the system commands are structured. This means that they only occur when the user becomes relatively skilled and then only intermittently. If this is correct then detection rates can only be improved by testing for a much longer period.

What this analysis has revealed is that a hard core of serious frequent and robust problems can be detected by any relatively inexperienced evaluator who has access to minimal training and only one naive user. But how does the performance of these students compare with that of specialist human factors evaluators?

Students and specialists compared

The list of twenty-nine problems generated by the students was compared with the inventory of known problems with REF. This inventory contained forty problems including all of the twenty-nine problems on the students' list. Of the eleven problems that the students failed to detect, seven were concerned with aspects of REF's functionality that was not covered by the student's task sheet, such as changing libraries printing and so on. The remaining 4 problems are listed in Figure 4.7.

As can be seen the problems all concern the user expectation of functionality that is not included in the REF system and may reflect the Cooperative Evaluation bias of a more sophisticated user population since much of the data for the REF inventory was gathered from professional computer users rather than naive users.

4.3.4 Discussion of Study 1: Improving cost-effectiveness

Synopsis

Q. How could we improve even further the cost-effectiveness of this technique?

A. In two ways. Give the evaluators more practice with the technique. They will get this naturally anyway as they do more evaluations. Secondly, test more subjects, but not too many; three or four users per iteration seems ideal.

Study 1 was intended to be a worse case assessment of the Cooperative Evaluation technique. Given minimal training and minimum access to users, how much information could a non-specialist obtain about an interface they

7b	the user expects a new selection to be displayed automatically
12d	the user expects a 'select-all' facility
12e	the user expects to have more than one 'current' selection
13b	the user expects to be able to browse both ways through a display

Figure 4.7
The scenarios detected by the authors but missed by the trainees in Study 1

did not even design? In this context the results are very encouraging. While the students who acted as our evaluators did not do as well as human factors specialists, and although there was a large degree of difference between them in terms of the number and kinds of problems detected, nevertheless all teams identified some serious problems with the REF system. In most cases the number of serious problems identified would merit the minimal investment of resources in order to mount and run a session.

Given the worst-case nature of this validation exercise, we were quite surprised by the effectiveness of the technique. It is worth considering, however, how the effectiveness of the technique could be improved without undue increase in investment.

Much of the investment cost involved in mounting a Cooperative Evaluation session lies not in the actual user testing but in the preparation of the system and task materials, and the training of the evaluators. Getting the system installed and running in a reasonably quiet environment and getting recording or logging equipment in place can involve considerable organisational effort. Likewise, preparing task materials and running through them on the installed system is time-consuming. The Cooperative Evaluation manual has been designed to minimise the effort required to read and understand it; nevertheless, familiarising oneself with the technique still requires several hours' work. But all these investment costs are non-recurrent and constant for whatever number of users are tested on a given application. So one easy way to consider improving the yield from a Cooperative Evaluation session is to consider what the effect would be of increasing the number of users tested.

By way of a thought experiment, consider the likely outcome of Study 1 if, instead of having thirteen teams of evaluators each testing one user, we had employed one evaluation team who tested all thirteen users. Would this have increased the overall number of problems detected, decreased it or left it the same? Without further empirical work the answer is not easy to provide. What we can say, however, on purely theoretical grounds is the following. Firstly, because the evaluators will have become more practised with the technique they are likely to improve in their ability to detect and understand the user's problems. Secondly, as the sample size tested increases so will the number of problems detected. Thirdly, and perhaps most importantly, the increase in the number of problems detected does not increase linearly with sample size. Rather there is a negatively accelerating curve which suggests that the greatest increase in the number of problems detected occurs between a sample size of 1 and 5. This is because the probability p_k of detecting a problem in k independent attempts, is given by:

$$p_k = 1 - (1 - p_1)^k$$

(where p_1 is the probability of detecting it in one attempt). As Figure 4.8 shows, this probability approaches 1 very quickly. Even a problem that has only a probability of 0.3 of being detected in one attempt has a very good chance of being detected in four attempts.

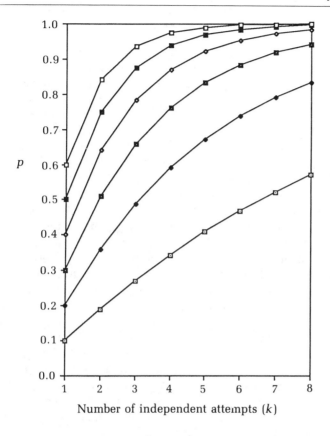

Figure 4.8
The probability (p) of detecting a problem in k independent attempts given some probability of being detected in one attempt (see intercept with ordinate) (from Wright and Monk, 1991a, see Bibliography)

Number of independent attempts (k)

If the assumptions of this theoretical model are correct, we would expect there to be a significant increase in the number of problems detected by an evaluation team if instead of testing one user they tested five. This represents an increased investment of only 5 hours of time for a large increase in the effectiveness of the technique. This 5 hours would represent a reasonable increase given the effort invested in installing the software and preparing for testing.

4.4 Study 2

Synopsis

Q. Can Cooperative Evaluation be used effectively by designers to evaluate interfaces they themselves have designed?

A. Yes it can. In this study we show how designers can use the technique to evaluate their own interface designs. We also find that they discovered usability problems which they did not expect.

4.4.1 Introduction to Study 2

There are two common objections to the suggestion that designers should carry out evaluations of their own designs. The first is that they will be over-protective towards their designs and fail to acknowledge usability problems. This, it is argued, would stem from the fact they have invested a lot of emotional and physical effort into the design and consequently do not like to see it criticised. The other objection is that designers do not need to carry out evaluations because, having designed the system, they already know what the usability problems are.

In consideration of both of these objections it is worth drawing a partial analogy with a general problem in software engineering. It is well known that the person who finds it most difficult to spot bugs in code is the person who wrote the code. Writing software tends to produce a tunnel vision and although the author may be able to identify and rectify obvious problems, the more subtle problems and difficulties often require a fresh eye if they are to be detected. For this reason many organisations structure their design process around software review meetings where several software engineers, including some not directly involved in the design, meet to discuss the code. The coordinator of the meetings manages them in such a way that the code authors do not feel that they personally are being appraised and criticised but rather that this is a normal part of the software validation practice.

Similar difficulties to those described above occur also in the design of the human interface. As mentioned in Chapter 1, a commonly cited problem for interface designers is that their view of a user interface is often quite different from that of the user. This means that their understanding of the system is often quite different from that of the users. Users often know more about the application domain than the designers, but often know less about how to use computers and how computers work. Furthermore their understanding of this is often heavily influenced by other applications they have used. One author, Donald Norman, refers to this state of affairs as a conceptual mismatch between designer and user. He argues that this mismatch makes it very difficult for designers to anticipate the problems that their users will have. While the interface they design might meet the needs of the designer, it does not meet the needs of its end users. Norman goes into this in some detail in a chapter called 'Cognitive engineering' published in a book by Norman and Draper (1986). More details are provided in the Bibliography for the interested reader.

Another researcher, Ankers Jørgenssen, has also done some work on this topic. In an experiment that he carried out, he ran a course for commercial designers and developers, and taught them how to use a think-aloud method very similar to Cooperative Evaluation. He then followed up these designers after they had used the technique to evaluate some applications they were working on. In interviews most of the designers said that the technique was very useful, that they were 'taken by surprise' by the kinds of difficulties their users experienced. Jørgenssen has reported this work in a paper called

'Using the think-aloud method in systems development' (Jørgenssen, 1989). The interested reader is referred to the Bibliography for more details.

It is important that evaluation should not be seen as criticising the designer's abilities. As in the case of the software review meetings, it is important that the organisation nurtures a view that user testing is not seen as implying a failure to design interfaces correctly. Rather it is a way of allowing the evaluator to gain a fuller understanding of the user's requirements, and this is best done first-hand in a cooperative and supportive environment. By presenting Cooperative Evaluation as a technique in which designer and user evaluate a prototype together, we have attempted to foster the right kind of environment for constructive evaluation.

The primary aim of this second study is to show that designers can use Cooperative Evaluation to evaluate their own designs. We also wish to demonstrate that a designer using this technique will discover more problems than would otherwise have happened. To this end we asked our designers to predict the usability problems they would expect to emerge in a user-testing situation. We compared the designers' predictions with what they actually found out. Finally, we wish to demonstrate that a designer evaluating their own interface is at least as effective as an equally experienced evaluator who was not involved in the design. In order to do this we will compare the performance of two groups of evaluators testing the same system, one group who have designed the system and one group who have not.

4.4.2   Details of Study 2

Synopsis

Q. How did you test these ideas?

A. We got some student software engineers to design a paper simulation of an electronic form filling interface. We then taught them how to use Cooperative Evaluation and got them to evaluate the designs. Some students evaluated their own designs while some evaluated other people's designs. We then looked to see whether the people who evaluated their own design did better or worse than the others. We also compared their predictions with the usability problems they actually observed.

There were thirty-two students in this second study and they formed themselves into sixteen teams of 2. The students were given the task of using Cooperative Evaluation to identify the usability problems in a prototype design.

As with Study 1, students were given the Cooperative Evaluation manual to study for one week before being provided with a single naive user for one hour. But unlike Study 1, instead of being given an existing system to evaluate, in this study they were asked to design their own prototype system.

Each team designed a paper-based prototype of an electronic touch-screen data-entry system, either a system for collecting data from applicants to be the first British cosmonaut, or a similar system for applications to a computer dating agency. Input was to be by means of a stylus used with a touch screen. The information to be sought was specified as a set of ADA data structures along with constraints on the display and the stylus input to be used.

The students were limited to a 22 × 31 character screen, represented by squared paper. They were told that each square could be blank, have a character in it and/or a border round it or part of it. They were told that squares or groups of squares with borders round them were designated as 'active areas'. The other areas were 'inactive areas'. They were told that when a user touches an active area with a stylus this would cause an ADA routine to be run, causing a change to the display or preparing the system for the user to write characters to the spaces in the active area. They were told that when the users touched an 'inactive' area nothing happened but that inactive areas can contain characters. They were then given the following details about active areas.

> When a user touches a square, in an active area, its location is reported to the main program, this alone can be used to signal an input, e.g. you might have two active areas one labelled 'male', and one labelled 'female'. Touching one sends the participant's sex to the main program. This kind of area will be called a 'button'. Alternatively, the user may be required to write into an active area, e.g. an empty box labelled 'age' may be supplied. It is assumed that input is complete if the user has made no further screen touches in that active area for 3 seconds. This obviates the need for an explicit <Enter> or <Return> key. This kind of active area will be called a 'field'.

Apart from these constraints the designers were free to collect the data in any way they saw fit. Many chose to use standard named buttons and fields, a few chose to use graphic icons. For the purposes of our study, four of the 'computer dating' designs and four of the 'British cosmonaut' designs were selected randomly. These were all evaluated by their designers one week after

Figure 4.9
Summary of the experimental design in Study 2. T1 is team 1, who produce cosmonaut design 1 (C1). T5 is team 5 who produce dating design 1 (D1), and so on

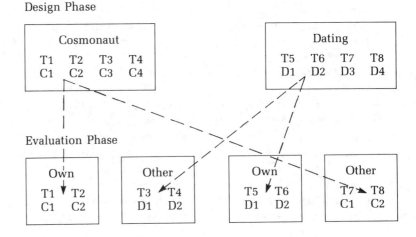

completing the designs. In addition each of the computer dating designs were evaluated by a team who had previously designed a cosmonaut interface and each of the cosmonaut designs were evaluated by a team who had designed a dating interface. Thus eight teams evaluated their own design and eight teams evaluated a design that was new to them. The procedures are summarised in Figure 4.9.

The above procedure allowed us to compare the performance of the eight teams who not only evaluated but also designed the interface with that of eight similarly experienced teams evaluating the same (i.e. someone else's) interface. This made it possible to see how the actual designers would compare with the actual evaluators. In addition we asked the designers who were evaluating their own interface to predict the problems their users would have. This made it possible to see how good the designers were at predicting the problems of their users.

4.4.3   The results of Study 2

Synopsis

Q. How well did the designers who evaluated their own designs do?

A. They did very well. They detected more problems than the others who weren't evaluating their own interfaces. Furthermore the problems they actually observed were quite different from the ones they had expected would occur.

How did the designers compare with the others?

The usability problems that we will concentrate on in this analysis are those directly related to design issues. There were others reported such as those related to problems with using paper and pencil prototypes, for example. But these are not central to our main concern here, which is can designers use the technique to detect design flaws? (For further details of the problems discarded see Wright and Monk, 1991a.) Most of the remaining problems concern difficulties in recovering from input error and ambiguities in input prompts.

The mean number of problems detected by the designers was 3.9 ($s = 1.36$) compared with 1.9 ($s = 1.62$) for designers not involved in the design. This difference was significant with a Mann−Whitney U-test ($U = 8, p = 0.005$). Thus it would appear that designers are better at detecting problems in their own design than in someone else's.

How well did the designers predict problems?

Designers are not, however, very accurate at predicting what problems they will observe. Although the mean number of problems predicted by the designers

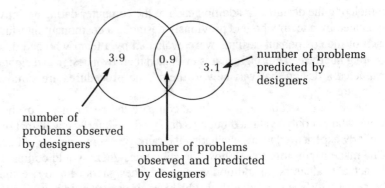

Figure 4.10
Mean number of
problems predicted
and observed by the
designers in Study 2

was very similar to the number observed, the overlap was very small. Few of the problems predicted by the designers were actually observed. Designers predicted a mean of 3.9 problems, but of those problems only 0.9 were actually observed. So the problems observed were quite unexpected. The non-designer teams performed similarly. Of the problems observed by the non-designers, only 0.5 had been predicted by the designers. These results are summarised in Figure 4.10.

4.4.4 Discussion of Study 2

Synopsis

Q. Is it useful to get designers to do their own evaluations?

A. Yes it is. They can use Cooperative Evaluation to discover problems in their designs and these problems are different from the ones they would have thought of otherwise. It is remarkable to find just how often users have difficulties with designs that we, as designers, thought were foolproof.

The results of this validation study clearly support our claim that designers can use Cooperative Evaluation to evaluate their own interface designs. Designers who designed and tested their own interfaces detected a significantly greater number of problems than similarly experienced designers who had not been involved in the design of the interface they tested. There are two very good reasons why this is so. Firstly, designers who are evaluating their own interfaces are better motivated to improve the design and to produce a better finished product. Secondly, designers who evaluate their own design understand that design better than anyone else. They are thus more able to recognise difficulties and potential pitfalls of their user's actions.

The study also showed that the usability problems that designers expected to find were not those that actually occurred during testing. This provides empirical support for the commonly held belief that the designer's model of the user is not an accurate one.

An alternative explanation of this observed mismatch is that user testing was not sufficiently thorough and that if more testing was carried out the problems predicted by the designers would begin to appear. This may be the case, and in the discussion of Study 1 above, we argued for the cost-effectiveness of increasing the number of users tested. This alternative explanation serves only to reinforce the need to supplement designer's intuitions about usability with evidence from user testing. By testing only one user the designer can usefully supplement their own understanding of the potential usability problems in the design.

Whichever way the finding is interpreted, it lends credence to the view that if designers and users are brought closer together, the conceptual gap between them can be narrowed and better products will ensue.

4.5   Summary and conclusions

Synopsis

Q. So what have we learnt from these laboratory experiments?

A. We have learnt that people without specialist human factors knowledge can use Cooperative Evaluation and that designers can use it effectively to gain often surprising information about problems with their own designs. It is this information that is most useful in making a design more usable and hence successful.

The aim of this chapter was to provide some quantitative evidence to validate two claims about Cooperative Evaluation:

* that Cooperative Evaluation can be used by non-human factors specialists
* that designers can use Cooperative Evaluation to evaluate their own designs

Study 1 showed that a group of non-specialists who had received minimal self-instruction on the Cooperative Evaluation technique could detect a reasonable proportion of the usability problems identified by a human factors specialist. While there were large differences between the number of problems detected by individual non-specialists, this is probably attributable to differences between users tested. Nevertheless, there were a robust set of usability problems that nearly all evaluators detected. The detection of these alone merits the minimal investment required to mount a Cooperative Evaluation exercise.

A theoretical model was put forward to suggest that the technique could be made more cost-effective by increasing the number of users evaluated from 1 to 5. This represents an increased investment of only 4 hours for a large increase in the number of problems detected. The model suggests that testing more than 5 subjects yields diminishing returns.

Study 2 showed that designers could use Cooperative Evaluation to evaluate their own interface designs. These designers detected more usability problems than designers who had not been involved in the design. The problems that were detected by using Cooperative Evaluation were different from the ones that the designers had predicted would arise, hence Cooperative Evaluation is a valuable tool in narrowing the conceptual gap between designers and users.

The two validation studies reported here are intended to provide quantitative evidence about the effectiveness of the Cooperative Evaluation technique and its usability as a tool for designers. They were not intended to be especially representative of how Cooperative Evaluation might be used in a commercial environment. But the results of these two experiments, taken together with the experiences reported in Chapter 3, provide a strong support for the belief that Cooperative Evaluation is a cost-effective technique that can be used by designers in a commercial setting.

Appendix 1   Cooperative Evaluation: a run-time guide

A1.1   Introduction

A1.1.1   What is Cooperative Evaluation?

Cooperative Evaluation is a procedure for obtaining data about problems experienced when working with a software product, so that changes can be made to improve the product.

A1.1.2   Who uses Cooperative Evaluation?

Cooperative Evaluation can be used by designers without specialised knowledge of human factors research.

A1.1.3   When to use Cooperative Evaluation

Cooperative Evaluation is most useful for early feedback about redesign in a rapid iterative cycle. The aim is not to provide an exhaustive list of all the problems that could possibly be identified. Rather, it is to help you identify, with the minimum of effort, the most important problems to consider. Cooperative Evaluation can be used with:

- an existing product that is to be improved or extended;
- an early partial prototype or simulation;
- a full working prototype.

A1.1.4   About this guide

This guide is intended as a 'stand alone' reference guide to Cooperative Evaluation. It is intended to help you prepare and run a Cooperative Evaluation session. It is *not* a detailed description of the technique, this can be found in Chapter 2. Rather it is a series of questions, summaries, reminders and checklists for each stage of preparing and running a session. We suggest that the best way to use this guide is to photocopy it and use the checklists when appropriate as you progress through the procedure.

The guide is divided into the three steps discussed in Chapter 2. These reflect the main activities of preparing and running an evaluation session.

- **Recruit users**
- **Prepare tasks**
- **Interact and record**

A1.2   Recruit users

A1.2.1   Define the target user population

Before you can say whether someone is typical or atypical of the eventual users of the product you have to define who those eventual users will be. If the product is to be used by a specified department or group of individuals then the existing employees define this population. Simply write the name of the group in the box below. The development of more generic products will be preceded by market research which will specify the user group. Even if the population is not defined for you, make an explicit decision to aim at some target user population.

> *Who are the eventual*
> *end users of this product?*

A1.2.2   Recruit users who are as similar to the target user population as is practical

We suggest you work with between 1 and 5 users per iteration early in the design process. Precisely how many will depend on practical requirements such as: how much time you have, how long it will take to run each session (see Prepare Tasks below) and how much time your users have.

> *How many users will you*
> *work with?*

Where you get your users from will depend on who you have specified as the target user population in A above. The table below suggests some possibilities.

Target population	Suggested source of users
A specified company, department or group of people	Ask the company, department or group
The general public	Advertise in newspapers
People with specific experience or skills	Use recruitment or secretarial agency
Don't know	Make up a 'user profile' and recruit people who fit the description

A1.2.3   Things to watch out for during recruitment

1. If you are NOT recruiting directly from an identified group, have you checked that the people you recruit have the same characteristics as your target users? Important considerations are:
   - Their knowledge of the task domain
   - Their experience of computers
   - Their skill at using keyboards and other input devices
   - Their level of education and how they will approach situations that require problem solving
2. Do you need to make arrangements to pay users? Do you need to seek permission for them to take time out of their normal work?

Where will you get your users from?
Whose permission will be required?
What administrative arrangements will need to be made?

Notes

A1.3   Prepare tasks

Selecting the right tasks is crucial for the success of Cooperative Evaluation. They must be do-able by the users, they must be representative of real tasks the users do and they must explore the prototype thoroughly.

    The aim of this step is to prepare a task sheet. This will contain a list of tasks that all your users will attempt to work through with your prototype. The task sheet is given to the user at the beginning of the Cooperative Evaluation session.

QUESTIONS TO ASK YOURSELF	
Questions	Answers and comments
Have you made sure that the tasks you have planned can actually be done using your prototype?	
Are they going to focus the user on the parts of the prototype you are interested in?	
How much time have you allowed for each user in total?	
How long do you estimate it will take each user just to complete the tasks?	
Is the total time you have allowed at least 50% greater than the time to complete the tasks?	
Have you written down the tasks in a way that can be understood by a novice user?	

A1.3.1   Things to watch out for when preparing tasks

1.   Are the tasks specific? 'Do your normal work' is not a specific task. 'Draw a house with a door, four windows and a chimney' is.

2. How do you know that the tasks you have chosen are representative of the work the product is designed to support? You may have talked to users about their job, you may have spoken to market research or other specialists in the company.
3. What are you going to do if the user cannot finish a task or if a user finishes too quickly? You may want to decide on a maximum time for each task. You may want some extra tasks up your sleeve that are easier or that can be given to people who finish more quickly than you expected.
4. Important functions should be examined twice, once at the beginning and once at the end of the session.

Notes

A1.4   Interact and record

This section is divided into four parts, telling what you need to do:

- Before the users arrive
- When the users arrive (before starting the tasks)
- While the users are using the system
- Debriefing the users

A1.4.1   Before the users arrive

Everything needs to be in place, tested and fully operational. Use the following two checklists. The first lists all the things you need. The second lists everything you should have done.

Have you got the following?	Answers and comments
Your prototype ready to use in a reasonably quiet environment?	
A sheet containing the user's tasks?	
Some means of recording what the user says, ideally a clip-on microphone plugged into the video recorder? (see below)	
Some means of recording what the user does (i.e. a video recorder or a system logger)?	
A notebook or proforma sheet on which to make notes?	
A list of questions to ask during debriefing?	

Have you done the following?	Answers and comments
Planned what you need to say when the user arrives? (see next section)	
Worked through the task sheet yourself so that you know what to expect?	
Checked that the recording apparatus is working correctly?	

Notes

A1.4.2   *When the users arrive*

The whole session should be conducted in an informal manner and you and the users should discuss the system openly. They should be encouraged to think of themselves as coevaluators not as experimental subjects. They should be told that you are interested in the way the system *misleads them* rather than in the *mistakes they make*. They should be told you are interested in the things that *the system makes it hard for them to do* rather than the things that *they are unable to do*. This emphasises that it is the system that is being evaluated not the user. This will help the question—answer dialogue to flow easily.

When the users arrive and before they start work on the tasks there are five things you need to do.

1. Put the users at their ease.
2. Start recording the session. Do this early on in case you forget later.
3. Introduce yourself. Explain who you are and the purpose of the session in general terms. Emphasise that you are testing the prototype system not the user. Explain the philosophy of Cooperative Evaluation.
4. Explain Cooperative Evaluation. You will need to describe the technique of Cooperative Evaluation. Explain that what the user says will be taped and that everything is confidential.
5. Introduce the task sheet. Explain that the tasks are not a test, just a way of introducing the user to the various parts of this new system.

We think this part of the session is best done informally so we DO NOT recommend that you have a written set of instructions. But we included some written instructions below to give you an idea of what you need to say.

Sample instructions for Cooperative Evaluation

Thank you for agreeing to help with this study. Today we are going to evaluate the usability of a particular computer system called REF.

REF stores large numbers of references to academic works rather like the catalogues in a library. It can be used to search for things written on a particular subject, or by a particular author and so on.

The aim of the study is to find out how easy REF is to use by people like yourself. We want you to use it to help us find out what problems REF poses and how it could be improved.

We will give you some standard tasks to do using REF. The aim of this is to allow us to get some information about how REF supports this activity. We are particularly interested in situations in which REF encourages you to make errors in selecting commands and misleads you about what it will do. We are also interested in extra commands that would make the system easier to use.

To get this information we shall use a question-and-answer technique. This involves three things.

1. We want you to think-out-loud as you do each task, telling us how you are trying to solve each task, which commands you think might be appropriate and why, and what you think the machine has done in response to your commands and why. Think of this as you giving us a running commentary on what you are doing and thinking.
2. Whenever you find yourself in a situation where you are unsure about what to do or what effect commands might have, ask us for advice. If you ask us what you need to know we will suggest things for you to try but if you get really stuck we'll explain exactly what you have to do.
3. In addition we will ask you questions about what you are trying to do and what effect you expect the commands you type will have. This is simply to find out what problems there are with the system. During our conversations, we want you to voice any thoughts you have about parts of the system which you feel are difficult to use or poorly designed.

While you are doing this we will be noting down the problems you mention but in case we miss any we are going to audio tape our conversation. This recording will be anonymous and treated in confidence.

Remember it is not you we are testing, it is REF. We are interested in what you think so do not treat this as an examination. Treat it as a structured discussion about REF. Please feel free to say whatever you think about the system and the tasks you are given to solve.

A1.4.3   *While the users are using the system*

The two main things to remember to do when the users are actually carrying out the task are

> KEEP THEM TALKING!
> MAKE SURE YOU KNOW WHAT'S GOING ON!

1. Encourage the users to think aloud while using the system. This is best done by asking them to give you a running commentary of what they are doing and what's going on.
2. Ensure that there is a relatively continuous dialogue by asking appropriate questions whenever possible. A1.4.4 is a list of useful questions. These can be photocopied and used as a 'crib sheet' during the session.
3. Note each occurrence of unexpected behaviour and each comment on the usability of the system. You will not have time to make detailed notes. What you need to do is make a note of where on the tape the behaviour or comment occurred and a brief (possibly one word) description of what happened. A proforma for this is included at the end of this section. Do not let note taking interfere with the primary task of creating a dialogue with the user. Stop note taking rather than let this happen.

Unexpected Behaviour is where the users do something the designer did not intend them to do. For example, the user might type in an inappropriate sequence of commands or data.

Comments are subjective comments or evaluations of the interface. These can be both positive and negative ('It's nice the way you can do that without having to type the whole thing again', 'That seemed to take a lot of effort', 'I don't like having to do that twice' and so on).

A1.4.4   Some useful questions to ask during evaluation

- How do we do that?
- What do you want to do?
- What will happen if ...?
- What has the system done now?
- What is the system trying to tell you with this message?
- Why has the system done that?
- What were you expecting to happen then?
- What are you doing now?

A1.4.5   Debriefing the users

When the user has finished the set tasks you should spend some time talking about the session. Keep the tape recorder on during this time. Some very interesting comments emerge out of this part of the session. As well as discussing what each of you think are important usability problems you can also get some feedback about the Cooperative Evaluation session itself. Some useful questions to ask the user are included as A1.4.6. These can be photocopied and used as a prompt. These questions are, however, very general; you will probably want to ask some fairly specific questions of your own about specific aspects of the prototype such as menu names, default values and so on.

If you are testing many users or you want more formal feedback, it may be worth considering drawing up a simple questionnaire for the users to fill in. Be careful not to make it too long or complicated. A good example of such a questionnaire is included in Chapter 3 as Figure 3.3.

It is sometimes possible to see users a second time either individually or as a group. If this is possible it is very useful. It allows you the opportunity of clarifying your interpretation of important usability problems and also discussing possible design changes. It also serves a useful customer relations function bringing users and designers together for a round-table discussion. This is discussed in more detail in Chapter 3.

A1.4.6 Some useful questions to ask during debriefing

About the prototype

- What do you think was the best thing about the prototype?
- What do you think was the worst thing about the prototype?
- What do you think most needs changing?
- How easy did you find the tasks?
- *Specific questions about the prototype ...*

About Cooperative Evaluation

- Did you find the recording equipment intrusive?
- Were the tasks similar to things you currently do?
- How realistic did you find the prototype?

Sample proforma sheet for making notes

No.	Tape count	Unexpected behaviour or Comment
1		
2		
3		
4		
5		
6		
7		
8		
9		
10		
11		
12		

Appendix 2   Some transcripts of a Cooperative Evaluation session

A2.1   Introduction

The aim of this appendix is to provide the reader with some source data from a Cooperative Evaluation exercise. There are several possible uses for these data.

1. Browsing through actual transcripts of a Cooperative Evaluation exercise, although it is time-consuming, can be a useful way to gain a very direct impression of how the technique works and of the kinds of data it generates.
2. If you are a human factors specialist or manager interested in introducing the technique into your company, examples from these transcripts can be used as training material.

The transcripts are taken from a Cooperative Evaluation session run at York to evaluate a small PC-based database system intended for use by University students and staff. In order to make the transcripts understandable we take some time to explain the system being evaluated and the tasks given to the user. This includes descriptions of what the user sees on screen and what effects their input has. The task the user is trying to complete is described and the method the designer expected to be used is made clear.

With these two pieces of information it is possible for the reader to scrutinise the transcripts and discover unexpected behaviours and comments from the user about problems experienced with the interface. The transcripts themselves have been heavily annotated to help the reader spot these usability problems.

A2.1.1   Using the transcripts as training material

These transcripts have been used by the authors as training materials for workshops at several international conferences. The kinds of training activities that we have used them for are as follows.

1. We have taken extracts from the transcripts, omitting the evaluator's questions and replies, and asked trainees to discuss what they would have done or said if they had been the evaluator.
2. We have used them as scripts for role plays. We play the parts of user

and designer and we use a story-board version of the computer screens. We then act out sections of the transcripts and ask the trainees to spot unexpected behaviours and comments.

3. We have given the trainees the transcripts and asked them to make an inventory of usability problems and some recommendations for redesign.

A2.2   Overview of the system and the user

A2.2.1   The system

The system studied in these examples is a bibliographic database called REF. REF was designed at York University to allow academic staff and postgraduate students to maintain an up-to-date record of references to journal articles, book chapters and so on.

It runs on the IBM PC and is a menu-based system. The user makes choices from the menu by typing the first letter of the menu option. The system has several different libraries corresponding to databases on different topics. The user loads a library and then makes selections from the library.

The top level menu includes options for making a selection from a currently loaded library, inserting a new reference into the library, altering a selected reference and so on. This top level menu is depicted schematically in Figure A2.1.

In the first few transcript extracts the user is carrying out a task which required making a selection of a number of references. So the command that we are particularly interested in is the SELECT command.

Figure A2.1
The REF screen at the start of the user's task

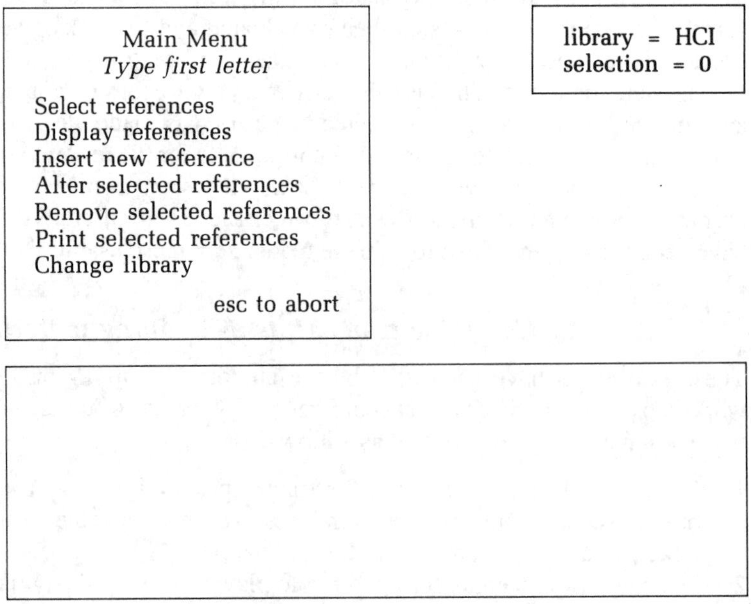

```
                Main Menu
              Type first letter

        Select references
        Display references
        Insert new reference
        Alter selected references
        Remove selected references
        Print selected references
        Change library

                    esc to abort
```

```
library = HCI
selection = 0
```

A2.2.2 Overview of the SELECT command

The selection command is an option in the main menu of the REF system (see Figure A2.1). It allows the user to search the database for a specific field value such an an author name, a keyword or a year of publication.

When the user inputs an 'S' to invoke the select command from the main menu, usually a sub-menu is presented offering a choice of three kinds of selection (see Figure A2.2).

1. If the user wants to get rid of the current selection and start a new one, they can choose the NEW selection option. To do this the user presses 'N' for new selection.
2. If the user already has a selection it is possible to add a new reference to it by choosing the ADD option. This is done by pressing 'A'.
3. If the user wants to make the selection more specific they can choose the REFINE option.

If the user has not already made a selection then the only available option would be to make a new selection. Such a situation makes this menu redundant. Anticipating this, the designer of REF does not present this menu if the user has not already got a current selection; instead the system jumps straight to the next menu described below.

After choosing any of the options from the menu depicted in Figure A2.2, the user is presented with the menu of fields which can be chosen to select by. This is depicted in Figure A2.3.

Once again the user simply types the initial letter of the field of interest.

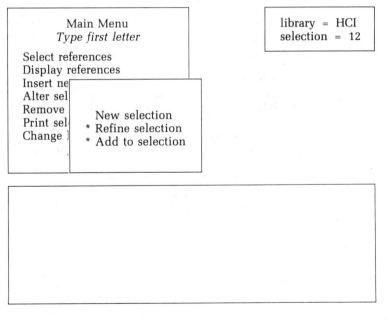

Figure A2.2
The REF screen after pressing S for select (previous selection)

Figure A2.3
The REF screen after
pressing S for select
(no previous
selection)

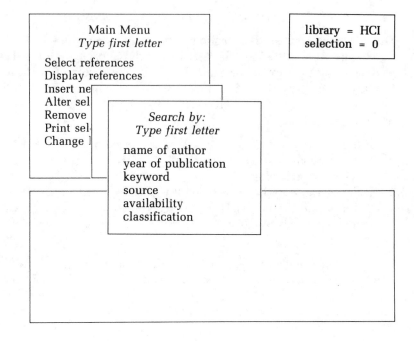

Figure A2.4
The REF screen after
pressing N for name
of author

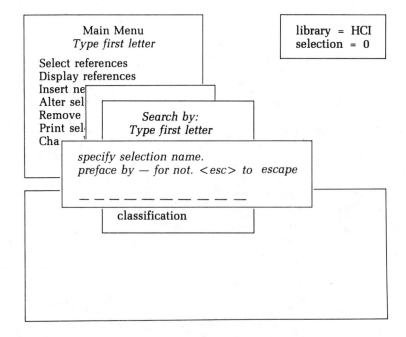

After choosing a selection field, the author is presented with a text entry field of the sort depicted in Figure A2.4.

In the case of the author field depicted in Figure A2.4 the user can type in a single author name followed by a < return > and REF will search the currently loaded library for references. If REF finds any references it will tell the user how many it has found by displaying the number found in the status box in the top right hand corner of the screen as in Figure A2.5. In addition if more than zero and less than four references have been found the references will be displayed to the user for browsing through the selection. In Figure A2.5, twelve references have been found so they are not displayed.

As can be seen in Figure A2.5, at the end of the search the system returns the user to the main menu so that they can refine the selection they have made perhaps by giving the system a second author or a date of publication.

In the transcript extracts you are about to read, the user has been given the task of finding a reference to a paper by Thomas and Gould written in 1984. To do this using REF they must first make a new selection and then search by the first author. Figure A2.6 summarises what the user should do. The user starts at the main menu as depicted in Figure A2.1 and ends with a selection of twelve items as depicted in Figure A2.5.

A2.2.3   The user involved in the Cooperative Evaluation sessions

The user who generated the transcript extracts in this appendix was a third-year PhD Student who had expressed interest in having access to a referencing

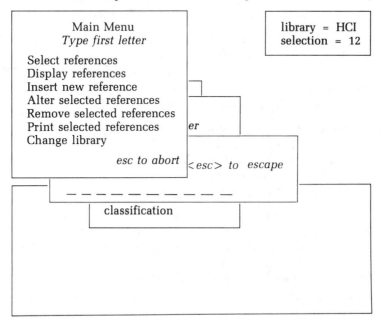

Main Menu
Type first letter

Select references
Display references
Insert new reference
Alter selected references
Remove selected references
Print selected references
Change library

esc to abort   <*esc*> *to escape*

er

classification

library = HCI
selection = 12

Figure A2.5
The REF screen after 12 references have been found

Figure A2.6
The correct dialogue
to search by the
author name Thomas
when there are no
previous selections

ACTIVE PANE	KEYSTROKES	COMMENTS
Main menu		
	S	invokes the selection menu
Search by . . .? menu		
	N	selects (N)ame of author as search field
Data entry field		
	Thomas <ret>	name of author followed by a carriage return
Main menu		search complete a new selection of 12 references has been found

system. She agreed to act as a user/evaluator of the REF system in exchange for a free copy of the software. She is fairly representative of the target population of REF, i.e. academics. She was conversant with statistics packages and Email on mainframe computers, had some experience of word processing on desktop systems but had little knowledge of computer science.

A2.3   The transcript extracts

The following five extracts are taken from this user carrying out the first task she was given to do with REF. Although we have split the transcript into five separate extracts, as you will see from the line numbering, the extracts are contiguous.

The transcripts adopt the following conventions:

- Every line is numbered for easy reference purposes
- User's talk is reproduced in plain text
- Evaluator's talk is in italics
- Comments by the authors are in normal text but are not numbered, or inserted into numbered lines in bold

The authors' comments serve several purposes. They explain what the system is doing, they point out unexpected behaviour or user's comments about the interface and they highlight any points of general interest. We have also provided an extended commentary at the beginning and end of each extract.

The user's task is presented at the beginning of Extract 1. References to schematic representations of the REF screens have been included at strategic points to help the reader work out exactly where the user is in the task. What the designer expected the user to do in order to complete her task has been described above in our overview of REF. Refer to this and especially Figure A2.6 for clarification if necessary.

Extract 1

TASK 1.   Find the title of the paper by Thomas and Gould 1974

In this first extract the user starts with no references selected and with the main menu as the active menu as depicted in Figure A2.1. The evaluator is expecting the user to type 'S' for select followed by 'N' for name of author.

1   Okay. Find the title of the paper by Thomas and Gould 1974
2   so S for select reference **[the user types an 'S']**
3   selection by, name of author, year of publication, keyword, what's it by Thomas and Gould
4   so I type the first letter so that's T . . . **[for Thomas]** no no it's not 'N' isn't it for name of author **[Unexpected behaviour]**
5   *That's good fine everyone makes that mistake*
6   *right*

In this extract the user starts by reading her task aloud (line 1). It is a good idea to encourage the user to do this because it helps when listening to the tapes later. At line 2 she announces her intention to press 'S' which she does, because she does not have a selection at present the system jumps to the menu depicted in Figure A2.3. At line 3 she reads the menu options. As can be seen from Figure A2.3, there is a prompt associated with this menu that tells the user to 'type the initial letter'. At line 4 the user does something unexpected — well almost. Instead of typing the initial letter of the menu choice she almost types the initial letter of the author's name. In our evaluations of REF this turned out to be a surprisingly common misunderstanding. In lines 5 and 6 the evaluator reassures the user and tries to put her at her ease, remember it's REF that is being evaluated not the user.

Extract 2

This extract continues from Extract 1, the user has arrived at the text entry field depicted in Figure A2.4. The evaluator is expecting the user to type in the first author name for her selection, i.e. Thomas. REF ignores upper/lower case distinctions.

7   Specify selection name. Do I need to use capital letters?
8   *No*
   [Unexpected behaviour: Here the user proceeds to type 'Thomas and Gould' but the system only accepts one author at a time]
9   Do I need to type 1974, no I'll just press return

At line 7 the user asks the evaluator a direct question. At this point the evaluator could have explored the user's assumptions a little further perhaps by saying 'what do you think?'. Instead he chose to answer her question directly because at this stage he did not want to get too involved with these low-level questions; he was more interested in finding out whether the user could get the basic task accomplished at all. At line 8 the user is doing something quite unexpected; instead of typing 'Thomas', the first author's name, she types 'Thomas and Gould'. At line 9 she asks the evaluator whether she needs to input the year of publication as well but answers the question for herself, and just presses return. The system is designed to read any text entry as a single string and searches for a reference with an author name that matches the string the user has input. Of course, it does not find any references and returns the user to the main menu with no references selected as depicted in Figure A2.1.

Extract 3

This extract continues from Extract 2. REF has just searched for a reference with the author name of thomas__and__gould and failed to find any references. The evaluator wants to explore what the user thinks has happened.

10 *Now what do you think it's done now?*
11 erm its looking for the reference so I would imagine I've got to now display, press display to see whether it
12 can display, the selected reference. Type the first letter which is D.
    [The user types D in order to display the selection]
13 What. Nothing's happened
    [The system didn't find anything so the menu refreshes and nothing is displayed]
14 *Why should that be?*
    [The user reads menu in search of a solution]
15 select a reference
16 display selected reference
17 insert new reference ... **[mumbles]**
18 perhaps it's not there. Perhaps it's not on file.
19 But it doesn't tell me it's not on file. **[Comment about the system]**
20 *It is on — it is there*
21 It is there.
22 *yeah*
    [She continues reading]
23 Print ...
24 *okay*
25 stuck
26 *stuck right erm*
27 unless it's on a different library. No it can't because it would say

At line 10, the evaluator asks the user to say what she thinks the system has done. This open-ended question is intended to elicit some information about the user's understanding of the unexpected behaviour. Her reply in line

11 reveals that she has not realised that REF has not found any references. In lines 11−13 she tries to display the selection and the system, much to her surprise in line 13, does not respond. At line 14 the evaluator tries another open-ended question to explore the user's understanding of the situation. At lines 15−18 the user reads the menu items trying to find some clue as to what is going on. The only thing she can come up with is that perhaps the reference she is looking for is not in the library (line 18). Her comment about the system in line 18 reveals that she has not seen the information in the status box in the top right hand corner of the screen (see Figure A2.1) that tells her it has not selected any references. Her belief that the reference is not there is a red herring that might distract from discovering the real problem (namely, that it searched for the wrong references), so the evaluator assures her the reference is on file in lines 21 to 22. She continues reading the menus and eventually gives up at line 25. The evaluator acknowledges this in line 26 and decides to intervene.

Extract 4

This extract continues from Extract 3. The evaluator decides to find out whether the user has seen the information on the screen that would help her work out what was going on.

[The evaluator points to the status window in the top right hand corner of the screen]

28 *Yeah. Erm this box over here.*

29 no references selected. Ah.

30 *This is a message box yeah. What do you think no references selected means?*

31 well I would have assumed, that it couldn't find it and one of the reasons that maybe it couldn't find it

32 is because its not in the library.

33 *okay. Well no references selected definitely means it hasn't found it. Erm.*

34 And I don't think I spelt it wrongly.

At line 28 the evaluator draws the user's attention to the status box and the fact it tells the user that there are no references selected. In line 30 the evaluator asks the user for any ideas about what this box means. For the rest of the extract the user tries to fathom out why there are not any references selected. Instead of telling the user what the problem is, the evaluator decides to ask the user to start the task over again to see whether she'll see what to do next time. In the next extract we rejoin the user after she has again tried a new selection and again typed in two author names.

Extract 5

Between the end of Extract 4 and the start of this extract, the user has started again on this task and once again, has typed in two author names. She is just about to do so again, when the evaluator decides that enough is enough.

40   *Okay let me tell you what's happening. In fact the machine only searches*
      by — can only take one author
41   *at a time.*
42   Okay so I just try Thomas. How do I delete?
      [The evaluator indicates the backspace key and the user deletes the
      second author name]
43   *Okay*
44   return
45   *Now what do you think it's done?*
46   References selected twelve. So I can . . . actually, its quite difficult to attend
      over at this top right hand corner of the screen **[comment about the difficulty**
      of attending to the status box in the top right hand corner of the screen]
47   because your attention's . . .
48   *Yes a lot of people don't notice that.*
49   I didn't notice it
50   *You'll find that when you get good at it you'll look at the screen even less*
      er and often
51   *you think it's selected references*
52   *when it's not*
53   *So what do you think it's done now?*
54   I think it's selected references so now I need to display references.
55   *Which references?*
56   Thomas' references, every Thomas reference.
57   Okay good.

At line 40, the user has typed in the two author names for a third time.
The evaluator is now convinced here is a real problem and decides to intervene.
At line 42, the user acknowledges the problem and realises she needs to delete
the last author. At line 44 she does this and presses return. At line 45 the
evaluator asks the user an open-ended question to check that the user really
understands what is going on. At line 46 she reads the status box in the top
right hand corner of the screen to see that there are twelve references selected.
She also makes a comment about the usability of this window saying that
it's very difficult to attend because your attention is focused elsewhere. Between
lines 46 and 52 the evaluator and user discuss this potential problem together.
Between lines 51 and 57, the evaluator checks with the user that she knows
precisely which references she has succeeded in selecting.

Extract 6

Having obtained all the Thomas references, the user is now back at the main
menu with 12 references selected as depicted in Figure A2.5. At this point
the evaluator expected her to choose the selection option again so that she
could refine her selection of 12. He was expecting her to refine by the second
author name which would have reduced the selection to 1 and displayed the
selection she was searching for automatically. Instead she decides to display
the twelve references

56 Type first letter, full reference or summary reference. I wonder what the difference is?
    [Comment: doesn't understand the display options]
57 Shall I type F for full reference.
58 *Okay*
    [The first of the 12 references is displayed in a window at the bottom of the screen]
59 Reference one of twelve. Thomas, J. and Schneider. So I need to press return to continue until I come to
60 Thomas and Gould **[Unexpected behaviour: Using the display option to search for the reference]**
    [Pressing return pages the user through the 12 references one by one]
61 These don't seem to be in alphabetical order
    [Comment: The references are displayed in the order in which they are inserted into the database not in alphabetical order]
62 *Good. That's great. No they're not.*
63 Thomas, J.C. and Gould, J.D. 1974. That — I mean there could be more than one of these couldn't there so
64 *How would you find out?*
65 I just have to keep going through won't I.
    [Because they are not alphabetically ordered the user must check all 12 references]
66 *It's a good idea to check.*
67 So really only to be able to specify the name of one author must be a severe limitation.
    [Comment: Indicates she hasn't realised the use of the refine command]
68 *There are ways round it which you'll find out.*
69 Because references are all — mean so much in terms of both authors' names that's how you tend to remember
70 them.
71 *Yeah.*
72 So this is the last one Thomas and Polson. So that's the end, erm.

At line 56 a comment reveals that she doesn't understand the display options but she chooses one anyway (line 57). Between lines 59 and 60 she declares her intention to browse through the references until she finds the one she's after. Using the display in this way is an unexpected behaviour. At line 61, she makes a comment that the references are not displayed in alphabetical order. The user clearly sees this as a usability problem and the evaluator discusses this with her between lines 61 and 66. Between lines 66 and 72, she indicates by her comments that she hasn't understood that it is possible to refine the current selection to achieve her goal of getting just the references by Thomas and Gould. She has, however, achieved her task of finding the reference by Thomas and Gould. Furthermore, she knows it is the one she wants because she has browsed right through the 12 references.

Bibliography

Gould, J.D. and Lewis, C. 'Designing for usability: key principles and what designers think', *Communications of the ACM,* **28**, pp. 300–11, 1985.

In this now classic paper the authors set out the principles of iterative design using users. The last part is a case study of the development of the ADS voice messaging system.

Gould, J.D., Boies, S.J., Levy, S., Richards, J.T. and Schoonard, J. 'The 1984 olympic message system: a test of behavioural principles of system design', *Communications of the ACM,* **30**, pp. 758–69, 1987.

This paper is a very readable account of the various prototypes and user testing procedures by which the authors developed the Olympic Message System, based on ADS (see Gould and Lewis, 1985).

Haber, J. and Davenport, L. 'Proposing usability testing to management — an "It works therefore it's truth" approach', in *Human Factors in Computing Systems: Reaching Through Technology, CHI'91 Conference Proceedings*, S.P. Robertson, G.M. Olsen and J.S. Olsen (eds), ACM, New York, p. 498, 1991.

This describes how Cooperative Evaluation was used at Information Dimensions Inc.

Jeffries, R., Miller, J.R., Wharton, C. and Uyeda, K. 'User interface evaluation in the real world', in *Human Factors in Computing Systems: Reaching Through Technology, CHI'91 Conference Proceedings*, S.P. Robertson, G.M. Olsen and J.S. Olsen (eds), ACM, New York, pp. 119–24, 1991.

Various evaluation methods were compared in this study of one user interface. Having usability experts evaluate it in an expert walkthrough (they confusingly call this 'heuristic evaluation') comes out as most cost effective. None of the groups has designed the user interface tested. User testing comes out as very expensive in time but they were not using Cooperative Evaluation.

Jørgenssen, A.H. 'Using the think-aloud method in systems development', in *Designing and Using Human–Computer Interfaces and Knowledge-Based Systems*, G. Salvendy and M.J. Smith (eds), Elsevier Science, Amsterdam, 1989.

A paper describing a questionnaire study of designers using a think-aloud technique.

Karat, C., Campbell, R. and Fiegel, T. 'Comparison of empirical testing and walkthrough methods in user interface evaluation', in *CHI'92 Conference Proceedings*, P. Bauersfeld, J. Bennett and G. Lynch (eds), ACM, New York. pp. 397–404, 1992.

The authors compare their evaluation of a user interface derived from watching people perform tasks with that of designers using Heuristic Evaluation. They conclude that in this situation Heuristic Evaluation is less cost effective. It is not very clear how this result would generalise as the user testing was done by expert experts (world authorities!) and the 'designers' had not designed the system evaluated.

Lewis, C., Polson, P., Wharton, C. and Rieman, J. 'Testing a walkthrough methodology for theory-based design of walk-up-and-use interfaces', in *CHI'90 Conference Proceedings; Empowering People*, J.C. Chew and J. Whiteside (eds), ACM, New York, pp. 235−41, 1990.

This paper explains the cognitive walkthrough technique for refining a design without user testing.

Nielsen, J. and Molich, R. 'Heuristic evaluation of user interfaces', in *CHI'90 Conference Proceedings: Empowering People*, J.C. Chew and J. Whiteside (eds), ACM, New York, pp. 249−56, 1990.

This paper describes the Heuristic Evaluation technique in which designers evaluate a prototype design with regard to a limited number of heuristic principles. Computer science students detect 51% of the problems in a teletext interface on average. They were not the designers of the system.

Norman, D.A. 'Cognitive engineering', in *User Centered System Design: New Perspectives on Human−Computer Interaction*, D.A. Norman and S. Draper (eds), Lawrence Erlbaum Associates, Hillsdale, NJ, 1986.

This is a very clear description of the problem of designing a user interface, from the point of view of a cognitive psychologist.

Rieman, J., Davies, S., Hair, C., Esemplare, M., Polson, P. and Lewis, C. 'An automated cognitive walkthrough', in *Human Factors in Computing Systems: Reaching Through Technology, CHI'91 Conference Proceedings*, S.P. Robertson, G.M. Olsen and J.S. Olsen (eds), ACM, New York, pp. 427−8, 1991.

This paper can be looked on as a follow up to Lewis *et al.* (1990) as it describes an automated version of the form-based evaluation procedure used in the former paper.

Whiteside, J., Bennett, J. and Holtzblatt, K. 'Usability engineering: our experience and evolution', in *Handbook of Human−Computer Interaction*, M. Helander (ed), North Holland, pp. 791−817, 1988.

This is an extremely useful reference paper. In the first part the authors specify their 'usability engineering' procedure in some detail. In the second half they describe and justify contextual enquiry.

Wright, P.C. and Monk, A.F. 'Evaluation for design', in *People and Computers 5*, A. Sutcliffe and L. Macaulay (eds), Cambridge University Press, pp. 345−58, 1989.

This paper discusses the different kinds of data that can be obtained from users and compares their effectiveness for the purpose of refining a prototype design. It concludes that some kind of think-aloud data is necessary to detect a substantial body of usability problems.

Wright, P.C. and Monk, A.F. 'A cost-effective evaluation method for use by designers', *International Journal of Man−Machine Studies*, **35**, pp. 891−912, 1991a.

The first part of this paper examines the cost and effectiveness of different procedures for refining a prototype by user testing. The second part describes two experiments, described here in Chapter 4, designed to validate claims made about Cooperative Evaluation. These are that it is effective after minimal training and that designers are effective evaluators.

Wright, P.C. and Monk, A.F. 'The use of think-aloud evaluation methods in design', *ACM/SIGCHI Bulletin*, **23**, pp. 55−7, 1991b.

This paper is a brief account of the experiments from the above paper.

Index